DISCOVER · NATURE

in the
Rocks

Things to Know and Things to Do

Rebecca Lawton,
Diana Lawton, Susan Panttaja

with illustrations by Irene Guidici Ehret

STACKPOLE
BOOKS

550
L425d

Published by
STACKPOLE BOOKS
5067 Ritter Road
Mechanicsburg, PA 17055

Printed in the United States of America

Cover illustrations by Irene Guidici Ehret
Cover design by Wendy A. Reynolds

First Edition

10 9 8 7 6 5 4 3 2 1

Excerpt from *Desert Solitaire* by Edward Abbey used by permission of Don Congdon
    Associates, Inc.
Excerpt from *Geologic Time* by Don Eicher used by permission of Michelle Johnson.
Excerpt from *Wild to the Heart* by Rick Bass used by permission of the publisher,
    Stackpole Books.

Library of Congress Cataloging-in-Publication Data

Lawton,Rebecca, 1954–
    Discover nature in the rocks : things to know and things to do / Rebecca Lawton,
Diana Lawton, Susan Panttaja ; illustrated by Irene Guidici Ehret. — 1st ed.
        p.   cm.
    Includes bibliographical references.
    ISBN 0-8117-2720-3 (alk. paper)
    1. Geology—Popular works.   I. Lawton, Diana.   II. Panttaja, Susan.   III. Title.
QE31.L36   1997
550—dc21   97-6064
                                                                                CIP

For our children
and their great curiosity

CONTENTS

PREFACE

Imagine that you lived in a place and knew nothing about it—say it was a small town, and you had never explored the streets or walked in the surrounding hills. Or imagine that you lived in a busy neighborhood within a big city and knew none of your neighbors. Or that you lived on a farm and had never wandered out in the fields.

Your curiosity would probably get the better of you. You'd have to get out and explore, to learn as much as you could about your home.

We humans have always explored our world. We've explored places far and near, met new and different people, and observed strange plants and animals. We've dug up soil and earth looking for fossils and valuable minerals. We've climbed volcanoes to get a close look, even when it's been dangerous, collected samples of every different rock type we could find, and measured the cracks in the ground surface left by the tearing action of earthquakes. We've left no stone unturned in trying to discover secrets about the earth: How old is it? How are rocks made? Where can we find fossils?

People ask these and other questions out of inquisitiveness about our larger home, the earth. In this book we help guide the reader to some of the answers. The study of our world is a relatively young science, open to as many discoveries as you can make. Begin here, and let your imagination take you where it will among nature and the rocks. You may be the next to find a small or large clue to the earth's great secrets.

ACKNOWLEDGMENTS

We wish to thank our families, whose generous moral support made writing this book possible: Howard Ehret, Steve Ehret, all the Lawtons, Ann Panttaja, Mary Evelyn Panttaja, and David Templeton. We also appreciate the excellent philosophical and technical advice we received from professional geoscientists Mary Jo Heassler, Mike Malone, Jay Mosley, and Mike Taraszki. Computer whiz Larry Floyd assisted in recovering lost disk files. David Fore and Kent Julin offered encouragement throughout the project. Matt McMackin and Louise Teal inspired us to get started in the first place.

Special thanks to our editor, Sally Atwater, for her patience and encouragement.

INTRODUCTION

We encourage readers of *Discover Nature in the Rocks* to use their powers of observation. For that reason, this book includes activities and experiments to be performed both indoors and out. Each chapter begins with information about the earth and ideas people have had about it. Read the chapters in any order according to your interest. Following the text in each chapter are activities for families to do at home or outdoors, for teachers to have students conduct in the classroom or laboratory, or for advanced younger readers to do with some supervision.

Many activities in this book will interest and be safe for small children if an adult helper is involved. Each activity also can be performed by more advanced readers and will capture their imagination if they ask more questions as ideas of greater complexity come up.

Explore the resources listed at the end of the book. Gather the necessary tools listed in each chapter for viewing, collecting, and recording your observations. More than anything, come equipped with a healthy curiosity, a tool that is available to us all at no cost.

Use caution when performing the experiments. They have been tested, but mishaps can occur during any activity. The authors and Stackpole Books are not responsible for accidents that happen during the activities we describe. Use good old common sense combined with a healthy dose of safety consciousness: Wear safety glasses when needed, protect your hands with gloves, use a buddy system when exploring outdoors, and be careful of heat and cold. Have fun and don't get hurt!

CHAPTER 1

Minerals: Building Blocks

About five centuries before the birth of Christ, popular belief held that all matter consists of four primary substances: earth, air, fire, and water. A few great thinkers of the time, however, such as Democritus and Aristotle, argued against that fashionable but unsubstantiated belief. They experimented, observing several substances in containers at different temperatures. As they watched a substance's shape and appearance change with variations in temperature and pressure—becoming gas, then liquid, then solid—they concluded that matter consists of particles too small to see that shift and move under changing conditions.

For hundreds of years after the Greek experiments, few people accepted the notion that nearly invisible particles compose matter. But by the 1600s, because of experiments testing the theories of physicists Sir Isaac Newton, Christian Huygens, John Dalton, and others, most scientists agreed that a

In ancient times, people believed that all matter consisted of various combinations of earth, air, fire, and water.

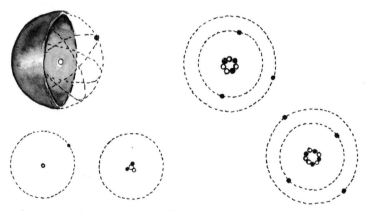

Each atom has a central nucleus—made of particles called protons—that is orbited by one or more electrons. The simplest atom, hydrogen, has a single proton for its nucleus orbited by one electron. Substances with more complex structures have more orbiting electrons.

DISCOVER NATURE IN THE ROCKS

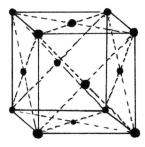

Copper has an isometric (cubic) structure, in which only atoms of the element copper are arranged in the orderly shape of a cube. The cubic structures aggregate to make a mineral, each cube having an atom of copper at each corner and in the center of each side, or face. The cube may have extra facets at each corner, giving it twelve sides rather than four.

basic particle, the atom, composes all substances and that it has a nucleus surrounded by subatomic particles, or electrons.

In a mineral, the solid phase of a nonliving, naturally occurring substance, atoms fill an orderly structure called a crystal. The crystal may be composed of one type of atom, or it may be made of molecules consisting of more than one type of atom. Native elements, which include the metals gold,

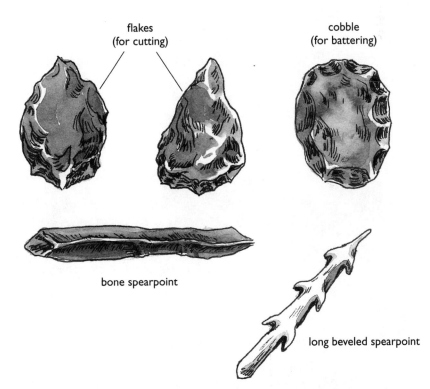

flakes
(for cutting)

cobble
(for battering)

bone spearpoint

long beveled spearpoint

Before the discovery of the metallic native elements for use in tool making, people fashioned tools from stones or bones. Stone Age tool makers knocked chips from stones to sharpen edges for scraping and ground down bone tips to shape spearpoints.

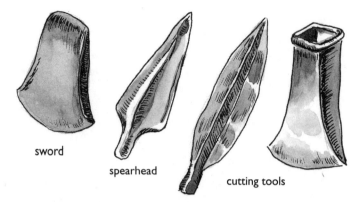

sword

spearhead

cutting tools

The use of bronze, a mix of the elements copper and tin, became popular between 3000 and 1185 B.C. (the Bronze Age). When early people discovered how to fashion tools and weapons from the element iron, around 1185 B.C., bronze fell out of favor and the Iron Age began.

The structure within the mineral pyrite has atoms of iron and sulfur arranged in a cubic shape.

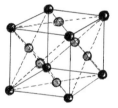

Pyrite is often found in cubic form, with striations, parallel lines of grooves, on its flat surfaces. Because of its golden color and metallic luster, pyrite is sometimes mistaken for gold. But gold is seldom found in its cubic form, even though its underlying crystal structure is cubic.

Instead, gold is most often found as irregular lumps laced through the mineral quartz.

Prospectors panning for gold learned the difference between gold and pyrite ("fool's gold") the hard way.

copper, and silver, are examples of single-atom minerals. Only gold atoms are in the native element gold; only copper atoms constitute copper. Pyrite, which resembles gold, is a mineral composed of molecules. Its cubic crystal contains both iron and sulfur atoms. It can be called by its mineral name, pyrite, or its chemical compound (molecular) name, iron disulfide. The mineral used for table salt is made of the atoms sodium and chlorine held together by mutual attraction. Salt has the chemical name sodium chloride and the mineral name halite.

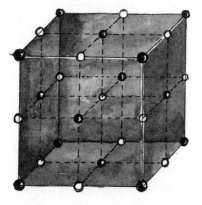

In salt, atoms of sodium and chlorine alternate in rows. This drawing of the structure of a salt crystal shows the atomic centers within the cubic form. In reality, the atoms, with their orbiting electrons, are large enough to touch each other. Salt was the first mineral to be explored and understood through the use of X rays, which probe into a crystal and expose its structure.

DESCRIBING MINERALS

At first glance, many minerals look alike, as do pyrite and gold. The clear crystal quartz, one of the world's most abundant minerals, may resemble another clear crystal called calcite, which is also abundant. But there are a few quick tests, based on how a crystal looks and feels, that you can use to tell even similar minerals apart. Each of the following properties is essential to describing minerals in the field or laboratory.

crystal system
habit
cleavage
fracture
hardness
specific gravity
color
streak
transparency
luster

Crystal System. More than twenty-five hundred types of minerals have been discovered on earth. Although their variety of shapes appears numberless, they actually fall into six basic categories of shapes, or crystal systems. Minerals crystallize, or grow, from liquid solutions, beginning with their central cores and building outward. At the mineral core is the shape of its molecule. In the mineral quartz, for example, atoms fill a hexagonal structure that joins with other, similar structures as it grows into a larger, six-sided crystal. Quartz is therefore assigned to the hexagonal crystal system, and it is often found in rocks as masses of hexagonal crystals.

Habit. Minerals have habits of growth, in which their crystals join together to form needles, blades, prisms, indefinite massive shapes, rounded kidney-shaped groups called reniforms, and feathery branchlike shapes called dendrites. The mineral beryl, which composes the blue-green gems emerald and aquamarine, has the habit of growing into huge prisms in rocks; the elemental

the six crystal systems

(drawn with graph paper lines to help visualize their shapes)

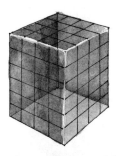

Isometric crystals are mainly cube shaped, but this system of mineral growth includes eight- and twelve-sided crystals as well.

A tetragonal crystal looks much like a cube but is somewhat longer than a cube in one direction (in this example, it is taller).

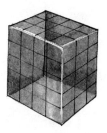

Orthorhombic crystals are classic prisms. Somewhat flattened forms are common in this system, as are other nearly cubic shapes that look a bit stretched or squashed.

The monoclinic crystal shape is more common than any other. Crystals in this system often have two sides that form at inclined angles to the others.

Triclinic crystals are not symmetrical: none of the sides mirror the others exactly. The faces and edges have no right angles.

A hexagonal or trigonal crystal is long in one direction and six-sided in its shorter direction.

habit, cleavage, and fracture

Silver is often found in wispy shapes called dendrites.

Beryl, the mineral more commonly known as the gemstones emerald and aquamarine, forms in columnar prisms.

The mineral calcite cleaves along weak planes to make beautiful rhombic pieces.

The conchoidal, or curved, fracture in opal.

mineral silver will rarely develop into crystals, growing instead in wispy, branchy dendrites.

Cleavage. When a mineral breaks, it usually splits along layers of weakness called cleavage planes. The cleavage planes may be between layers of atoms or in planes where atomic bonds are weak. A salt crystal, consisting of alternating rows of sodium and chlorine atoms, breaks neatly in perfect cleavage planes between the rows. Micas, which are platy, flaky minerals common in many types of rocks, have perfect cleavage between the layers, in thin sheets parallel to the mineral's base.

Fracture. Some minerals, when struck hard, do not break along clean and even cleavage planes. Instead, they break into pieces with rough surfaces. This breaking, called fracturing, results in different fracture surfaces: uneven, conchoidal (curved), hackly (jagged), and splintery. Sometimes a mineral breaks in a combination of ways, with cleavage planes on some edges and fractures where cleavage planes are absent. But some minerals simply fracture, leaving curved or jagged edges. The mineral opal consists of clusters of microscopic spheres of quartz. Dispersed among the quartz spheres are molecules of water. Because it has no well-defined crystal structure, opal, when broken, fractures conchoidally.

Hardness. A mineral's hardness is a measure of how difficult it is to scratch. Soft minerals can be scratched with your fingernail, whereas harder minerals cannot be scratched even with a knife. In the early 1800s, the German scientist Friedrich Mohs invented a scale for comparing hardness among rocks. The Mohs scale assigns the measurement 1 to the soft, easily scratched talc (the ingredient once used in many bath powders). The hardest-to-scratch mineral, diamond, has the measurement 10. Many other minerals, rated 2 to 9 in terms of hardness, fall between talc and diamond on the scale. A harder mineral can scratch a softer mineral. The minerals rated 1 to 5—talc, gypsum, calcite, fluorite, and apatite—can be scratched with a knife blade, which has the hardness of 5½. The minerals rated 6 to 10—orthoclase, quartz, topaz, corundum, and diamond—cannot. The hardness test is easy to use in the field because it requires no special equipment. Even nickels and dimes (hardness 3½) can help test whether a mineral is relatively hard or soft.

Specific Gravity. A mineral's specific gravity is a comparison of its weight with that of the same volume of water. Quartz has a specific gravity of 2.6, weighing just over two and a half times the same quantity of water. Two minerals with high specific gravities are the heavyweight native elements gold (19.3) and platinum (21.4). Some minerals with low specific gravities are

the Mohs scale of hardness

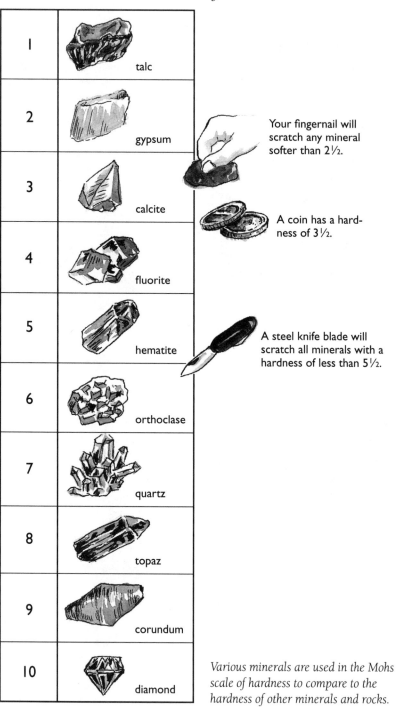

1	talc
2	gypsum
3	calcite
4	fluorite
5	hematite
6	orthoclase
7	quartz
8	topaz
9	corundum
10	diamond

Your fingernail will scratch any mineral softer than 2½.

A coin has a hardness of 3½.

A steel knife blade will scratch all minerals with a hardness of less than 5½.

Various minerals are used in the Mohs scale of hardness to compare to the hardness of other minerals and rocks.

sepiolite (2); graphite (2.1 to 2.3), which is the lead in pencils; and sulfur (2 to 2.1), which is often found as yellowish crusts in caves and hot springs.

Color. Color cannot always be trusted to help us tell minerals apart, because the same mineral can take on many colors. Quartz can be clear, rose, yellow, white, purple, or brown. Sapphire can be clear, green, yellow, or purple. On the other hand, different minerals may be the same color. Both gold and pyrite are pale yellow. Turquoise, the pale or bright blue-green mineral stone used in much jewelry making, can be confused with another blue-green mineral, chrysocolla. Color should be noted but not relied upon when naming a mineral.

Streak. When some minerals are rubbed on a porcelain tile, they leave behind smudges of color known as mineral streak. Streak is a better clue than color to a mineral's identity, because the streak is always the same for a given mineral, no matter what its outer appearance. Streak can be very different in color from the mineral itself. The gold-colored pyrite leaves a green-black streak. Blood-red rubies streak pure white. And quartz—which can be clear, white, gray, black, yellow, orange, red, pink, purple, brown, blue, or green— leaves an uncolored streak.

Transparency. A crystal's transparency is described as being transparent, translucent, or opaque. Transparent minerals, such as halite, quartz, and diamond, allow the passage of light and may be peeked through like windows. Translucent minerals allow light to pass through but cannot be seen through; many gemstones, such as aquamarine, ruby, garnet, amethyst, sapphire, topaz, and emerald, are translucent. Opaque minerals, such as gold, silver, and platinum, cannot be seen through even when cut very thin.

Streak is a reliable way to help identify minerals. When rubbed on a porcelain surface, minerals leave characteristic smudges, or streaks, of color. Any given mineral, no matter what its appearance, will usually streak a certain color.

Luster. Luster describes how light reflects off a mineral's surface. Luster can be pearly, dull, greasy, silky, or glassy (vitreous). Many of the gems—ruby, sapphire, beryl, amethyst, emerald, and topaz—have vitreous luster, giving them their brilliant shine. The common mineral gypsum, used to make plaster or cement, can have glassy, silky, or dull luster.

COMMON MINERALS

Some minerals, such as gold, platinum, silver, and copper, are not common but are of such economic importance or interest that they are well known. In contrast, other more common minerals are little known. Twelve are listed below; study them further in illustrated mineral handbooks such as those listed under "To Read" at the end of this chapter.

Quartz: One of our most common minerals, quartz is found in all rock types. It is composed of nearly pure silicon and oxygen; its chemical name is silicon dioxide, or silica. Quartz occurs as semiprecious gemstones or is deposited as microscopic crystals in light-colored veins that cut through rocks. It is often clear or white but can be almost any color and is recognizable by its distinct six-sided crystals topped by pyramids. Quartz crystal faces often show striations (parallel lines of grooves) such as are found on pyrite faces, and the crystals are often distorted in appearance. Quartz is not particularly dense, with a specific gravity of 2.65, but it is fairly hard (hardness 7). Well-formed hexagonal crystals that are clear or white and cannot be scratched with a knife are often quartz crystals.

Feldspar: Understanding feldspar begins with learning that it occurs almost everywhere, in most types of rocks. It comes in many varieties, with a wide range of chemical compositions, depending on the amounts of potassium, sodium, and calcium in its molecular structure, which also contains silica and aluminum. The most common potassium feldspar is orthoclase. Feldspars rich in sodium and calcium range from albite, with mostly sodium and a little calcium, through oligoclase, andesine, labradorite, and bytownite, to anorthite, with mostly calcium and a little sodium. Potassium- and sodium-rich feldspars are also called alkali feldspars. Feldspars are often light in color, but they can also be dark or even blue. They have hardness of 6 to $6\frac{1}{2}$, are triclinic and monoclinic, have perfect or distinct cleavage in two directions, and have uneven to conchoidal fracture. They are remarkable in that they are the essential components of many rocks.

Amphibole: Amphibole crystals are often found in rocks as long, prismatic crystals with a hardness of around 5 or 6. They can be dark in color or white to gray. There are many different types of amphiboles, with different chemical makeups—hornblende, anthophyllite, glaucophane, grunerite—in various types of rocks. Amphiboles have good to perfect cleavage in two directions and have striated prismatic to fibrous crystals with vitreous or silky luster.

Pyroxene: Pyroxene, like amphibole, grows in many different types—diopside, augite, and hypersthene, to name a few—distinguished by variations in molecular composition. Pyroxenes are often dark in color but, like amphibole, also can be white or gray. It takes a bit of study with a good mineral handbook to begin to understand pyroxenes, but they are common and important minerals in many kinds of rocks. Pyroxenes have good cleavage in two directions, hardness of around 5 to 6½, and uneven fracture. Pyroxenes are usually translucent to opaque.

Pyrite: Pyrite is called "fool's gold" for its golden yellow appearance, resembling the native element gold. It is found in all types of rocks, often as tiny square-faced crystals scattered throughout. Pyrite gives off sparks when struck with metal. Its crystal faces often have striations, parallel series of grooves or scratches, on their surfaces. Pyrite grows in many different habits but is best known as cubic crystals with striated (grooved) surfaces.

Halite: Halite, ordinary table salt, forms in salt lakes or lagoons as water evaporates. Halite dissolves in cold water, feels greasy when handled in larger crystals, and flames yellow when thrown onto a fire. Halite is soft (hardness 2)—you can scratch it slightly with your fingernail (hardness 2½). Halite has a low specific gravity (2.1 to 2.2), so it will feel light in your hand. It has perfect cubic cleavage; look for both cube-shaped crystals and cubic cleavage faces. Its fracture is uneven to conchoidal, contrasting fairly sharply with its cubic features.

Calcite: Calcite makes up most of limestones and marbles. It is contained in many rocks, in white, clear, gray, red, brown, green, or black crystals. Often it fills veins and holes in surrounding rock. It is transparent to translucent and soft (hardness 3). It can be distinguished from quartz, which is harder (hardness 7), by scratching with a coin (hardness 3½) or knife blade (hardness 5½). Calcite has perfect cleavage, with planes often visible on crystal surfaces. It is used to make cement, building exteriors, marble statues, and other decorative sculpture.

Gypsum: Soft (hardness 2), lustrous crystals of gypsum can be found around the edges of hot springs, where it is deposited out of evaporating water, or throughout beds of clay. It varies in color, from clear to white, gray, greenish, yellowish, brownish, or reddish. Gypsum streaks white. It can radiate in rosette-shaped clusters of crystals called gypsum roses, form transparent diamond-shaped crystals, or occur in tabular bundles of fibrous crystals.

Gypsum can be scratched with your fingernail. Gypsum is used in making plaster and wallboard for buildings.

Mica: Micas have perfect cleavage that parallels the base of their crystalline structures. Micas form in rocks in big clumps that can be peeled off by layers as if they were pages in books. Micas often have a clear streak, although the rocks themselves range from clear to white or gray through reddish brown and green, sometimes with metallic luster. Micas are characteristically soft, with a hardness ranging from 2 to 4, and in most cases can be scratched with a knife blade (hardness 5½).

Magnetite: This common black mineral composed of iron and oxygen atoms is highly magnetic, having the ability to attract iron filings or move compass needles. It is opaque and may be metallic or dull in luster. Magnetite leaves a black streak. It is in the cubic (isometric) system, and eight- and twelve-sided crystals are usual. A knife blade probably will not scratch a specimen of magnetite, which has a hardness of 5½ to 6½. Magnetite has no cleavage.

Rocks are clusters of minerals. This drawing shows how a massive cliff of granite, when viewed more closely, is composed of interlocking crystals that include the minerals quartz, mica, and feldspar.

Hematite: Another mineral composed of iron and oxygen, hematite ranges in color from blood red to iron black but always streaks red. It has many different habits and possible lusters, from brilliant metallic hexagonal crystals to dull weathered masses. It often replaces other minerals in areas where hot liquids have moved through a rock. Like magnetite, hematite has no cleavage. It has uneven to nearly conchoidal fracture. Both hematite and magnetite are important iron ores.

Galena: Galena is a very common mineral that forms in cracks in the earth where hot liquids have percolated up toward the surface. Galena is also known as lead sulfide, a compound made of lead and sulfur, and it is an important lead ore. It is soft (hardness 2½) and dense (specific gravity 7.58). Classified in the cubic (isometric) crystal system, it has perfect cubic cleavage that results in beautiful, well-formed cubes. Galena has a bright metallic luster.

As Democritus and Aristotle suspected, atoms and molecules compose all matter. In minerals, the atoms and molecules have crystallized as structures that are the building blocks of all rocks, which are simply clusters of minerals brought together under many different conditions of temperature and pressure.

TO DO

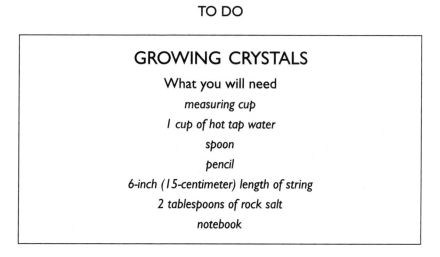

GROWING CRYSTALS
What you will need
measuring cup

1 cup of hot tap water

spoon

pencil

6-inch (15-centimeter) length of string

2 tablespoons of rock salt

notebook

Toy and hobby stores sell crystal gardens to grow, but crystals also may be grown without a kit. Growing crystals requires a small amount of rock salt, which is usually stocked in supermarkets near ordinary table salt.

Fill the measuring cup with hot water. Add the rock salt and stir the solution until the salt is dissolved. Tie the string around the pencil; rest the pencil across the top of the cup so that a length of string dangles into the salt water. Leave this crystal solution in a sunny place. Note the changes in solution and on the string over the course of days and weeks. Sketch your observations and describe changes in the solution as the crystals grow.

Explanation: Crystals grow out of solution when random bunches of atoms become ordered because of changes in temperature, pressure, and concentration. In this experiment, the water evaporates, leaving the sodium and chloride atoms in less water, thereby increasing their concentrations in the solution. As the water grows more salty, it can no longer hold all the salt in solution, and the salt precipitates and crystallizes. Slow evaporation results in the grouping of atoms into a few large crystals; faster evaporation activates the grouping of several small crystals on many centers of crystallization.

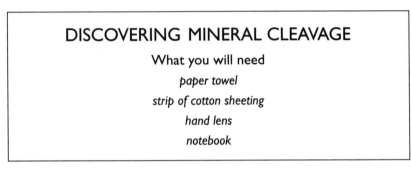

DISCOVERING MINERAL CLEAVAGE

What you will need

paper towel

strip of cotton sheeting

hand lens

notebook

This simple activity illustrates how cleavage works in minerals.

Rip a 6- to 8-inch (15- to 20-centimeter) wide strip of cotton shirt or bedsheet fabric in the direction that is easiest to tear. Cut the strip into 6- to 8-inch (15- to 20-centimeter) squares. Two edges of the fabric will be cut and two edges torn. Inspect the pieces of material with your hand lens. Can you see a pattern in the thread structure? Sketch the pattern in your notebook. Note on your sketch how the thread structure relates to the edges of the fabric.

Try to tear the fabric, first beginning at the torn edge, then beginning at the cut edge. Note your observations. Which direction was easier to tear? Think about the results of the tearing exercise and how other fabrics tear. What happens when you tear a hole in your pants or shirt? Does the cloth rip or tear in one direction? Two directions? All directions?

Next, inspect the paper towel. Using your hand lens, carefully observe the pattern in the paper towel created during its manufacture. Describe and sketch your observations in your notebook. Try to tear the paper towel, first beginning at the perforated edge, then beginning at the finished edge. Which direction was easier to tear? Note any sensations or sounds. Write down any similarities or differences between tearing the fabric and the paper towel.

Explanation: Minerals split easily and smoothly along cleavage planes, but not so easily in other directions. These cleavage planes often lie between layers of atoms, where atomic bonding is weakest and most likely to break apart. Any fabric, such as the cotton sheeting used for the tearing exercise, has a warp and weft. The warp is made of long, strong threads running the length of the fabric, and the weft is the filling thread or yarn that runs crosswise to the warp. Tearing across the warp is more difficult than tearing across the weft. Tearing lengthwise in the direction paralleling the warp is much like breaking a mineral along cleavage planes. Similarly, the paper towel has a preferred direction for tearing. The weaker bonds in the material's structure are most easily torn, leaving the stronger bonds intact.

It is interesting to note that some rocks show a strong pattern, called fabric, in their structures, which is similar to mineral cleavage.

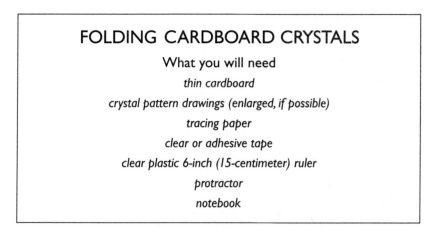

FOLDING CARDBOARD CRYSTALS

What you will need

thin cardboard

crystal pattern drawings (enlarged, if possible)

tracing paper

clear or adhesive tape

clear plastic 6-inch (15-centimeter) ruler

protractor

notebook

In this experiment, you can fold your own crystal shapes to create all six crystal systems.

Trace the crystal patterns onto tracing paper; add striations or markings as desired. Tape the traced patterns onto thin cardboard and cut out the shapes. Fold along the lines drawn, and fasten the edges with tape. You now have six crystal models, each representative of one crystal system.

Sketch the shapes in your notebook. If you wish to create varieties of any one shape, experiment—add new features. You can copy nature by creating variations in each system: cubic (isometric), tetragonal, orthorhombic, monoclinic, triclinic, or hexagonal.

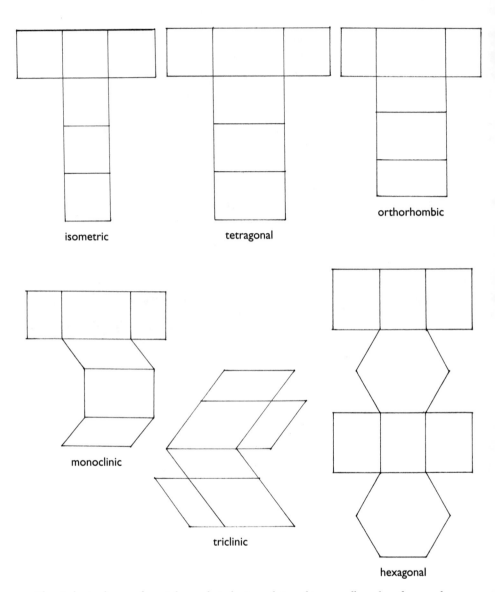

The six basic shapes of crystals, ready to be traced, taped to a cardboard surface, and folded into models.

Next, place your protractor on a flat surface (desk or tabletop) with the straight measuring side closest to you. Cross your ruler over the protractor, with an edge lined up on both the protractor's center dot (on the flat measuring side) and the 90-degree mark (on the curved measuring side). The ruler is now lying at a 90-degree angle to the straight measuring side of the protractor. Place one side of the cubic (isometric) crystal model against the plastic ruler edge and one side against the flat measuring side of the protractor. Because the sides of the model line up with the ruler and protractor edges, the angles you are measuring on the cubic crystal are said to be 90-degree angles.

Measure each crystal model the same way. Do they all have 90-degree angles, or do you have to move the ruler to other degree marks on the protractor? Determine what angles each crystal has and write the numbers in your notebook.

Explanation: Building your own cardboard minerals helps illustrate the six crystal systems. Remember that the basic shapes are only building blocks for thousands of different crystal shapes. The measuring and observing exercises should reveal that cubic (isometric) crystals have only right angles at their corners and all sides equal in size. Tetragonal crystals have only right angles and two different side lengths. Orthorhombic crystals have only right angles and three different side lengths. Monoclinic crystals are shaped as if they were orthorhombic crystals pushed into a slight slant; they have eight angles that are not right angles and eight angles that are. Flatten a monoclinic crystal so that there are no right angles and you will get a triclinic crystal, with no right angles and three different side lengths. Hexagonal crystals, on the other hand, have six sides, with right angles between each vertical side and the top and bottom and 120-degree angles between the vertical sides.

EDIBLE CRYSTALS

What you will need

clean hands

miniature marshmallows

toothpicks

notebook

This experiment illustrates atomic structures within crystalline shapes.

Using these materials, how would you begin to build a square? A cube? Try it. Using eight marshmallows and twelve toothpicks, build a model of a cubic (isometric) crystal. Using eight more marshmallows and twelve more toothpicks, build a tetragonal crystal structure. Will all the toothpicks for this model be the same length, or will you have to break a few to shorten them?

Sketch the models in your notebook before eating the marshmallows.

How might you build an orthorhombic crystal model of marshmallows and toothpicks? A hexagonal model?

Explanation: Your cardboard models showed the faces and angles in each crystal system, but your marshmallow models show how the atoms are held together by bonds into an orderly structure. In any mineral, such structures are regularly repeated, again and again, until the mineral grows larger, in a characteristic shape.

Collecting Crystals. Gathering your own collection of crystals is one of the best ways to learn about them. Read the "To Do" section of chapter 2 for helpful hints about making a rock kit; the same tips apply to collecting minerals and making a mineral kit. Be sure to follow the instructions with regard to collecting on private and government property, becoming aware of safety measures, and using the proper tools.

TO THINK ABOUT

Precious Minerals. A gem, or jewel, is a precious or semiprecious crystal, cut and polished for an ornament. Precious gems are valued at great price; semiprecious gems are less commercially valuable than precious but still treasured. People have always valued gem-quality crystals. In China in 900 B.C., people believed that jade—the gem-quality form of either of the minerals jadeite or nephrite—made them live forever; they constructed special suits of jade and gold to bury their dead. As recently as the eighteenth century, common thought held that sapphire could cure insanity, powdered jet (a compressed velvet black coal) could assuage toothache, and topaz could alleviate asthma. Today, some people wear quartz crystal pendants, believing them to have healing or cosmic properties. Other people wear amber beads to cure goiter. Still others believe opals bring bad luck. Can minerals heal our bodies and lives? Can they bring good or bad luck? Have you ever seen an instance in which a rock or mineral changed the course of someone's life?

Mineral Names. In his book *Desert Solitaire: A Season in the Wilderness,* Edward Abbey wrote: "The very names are lovely—chalcedony, carnelian, jasper, chrysoprase and agate. Onyx and sardonyx. Cryptocrystalline quartz. Quartzite. Flint, chert and sard. Chrysoberyl, spodumene, garnet, zircon and malachite. Obsidian, turquoise, calcite, feldspar, hornblende, pyrope, tourmaline, porphyry, arkose, rutile. The rare metals—lithium, cobalt, beryllium, mercury, arsenic, molybdenum, titanium and barium."

The names of rocks and minerals may not be all important, but they both delight and inform. Often minerals are named for the scientists who first recognized them or the locations in which they were discovered. Some names have other meanings. As you explore the rocks, consider the mineral names for both their beauty and the clues they offer: chrysocolla, antlerite, labradorite, rhodochrosite, psilomelane, talc, cinnabar, calaverite, bismuth, goethite, corundum, chromite, spinel, and celestite.

TO READ

Chesterman, Charles. *The Audubon Society Field Guide to North American Rocks and Minerals.* New York: Alfred A. Knopf, 1978. This excellent guidebook has color photographs of rocks and minerals, as well as full descriptions and informative text.

————. *The Audubon Society Pocket Guides: Familiar Rocks and Minerals.* New York: Alfred A. Knopf, 1988. This pocket-sized guide is a handy, condensed version of the larger Audubon field guide.

Hanauer, Elsie. *Rocks and Minerals of the Western United States.* New York: A. S. Barnes and Company, 1976. Maps and state-by-state hints on finding good specimens make this a practical guide.

Pellant, Chris. *Rocks and Minerals.* New York: Dorling Kindersley, 1992. Beautiful illustrations and interesting facts about various minerals fill this book.

Stangl, Jean. *Crystals and Crystal Gardens You Can Grow.* New York: Franklin Watts, 1990. Experiments in crystal growing are illustrated with clear photographs and line drawings.

Zim, Herbert S., and Paul R. Shaffer. *Rocks and Minerals: A Guide to Familiar Minerals, Gems, Ores, and Rocks.* New York: Golden Press, 1957. This pocket-sized classic is handy to carry on trips and while exploring outdoors.

TO WATCH

Crystals: They're Habit Forming. Children's Television Workshop, 1991. This film includes instructions for crystal-growing experiments.

Gold in Modern Technology. United States Bureau of Mines, 1987. This video explores how the mineral gold fits in our everyday lives and modern technology.

Prosperity Is a State of Mines. California Mining Industry, 1985. This video looks at some minerals we use every day and explores mining-related issues of conservation and environmental preservation.

CHAPTER 2

Rocks:
Pieces of Earth

Every rock on the earth's surface is part of the crust, a layer of rock that rings the globe. The crust varies in thickness from about 3 to 42 miles (5 to 70 kilometers) and resembles the thin pastry covering on a hot pie. If the world were the size of an 8-inch (20-centimeter) pie, the crust at so small a scale would be much thinner than even the most delicate of pastry crusts—as thin as fine thread. Beneath the crust lies the mantle, an approximately 1,900-mile (3,000-kilometer) thick layer of rock so hot that it oozes and flows. In the center of the earth is a white-hot core of iron and nickel. Some scientists have likened the earth to a globe of brewing soup covered by a thin floating layer of scum. In reality, although the soup description is useful, the inner earth is semimolten rather than truly liquid, and the crust does not float or move about as freely as scum on a pond.

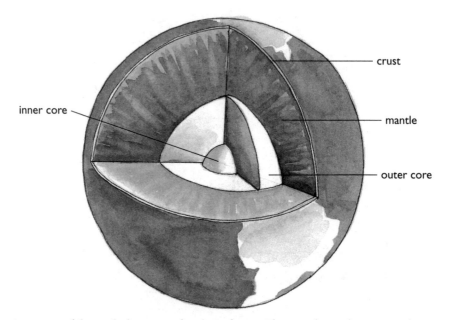

inner core

crust

mantle

outer core

A cutaway of the earth showing its four inner layers. The outer layer, the crust, is about 3 miles (nearly 5 kilometers) thick beneath the world's oceans and more than 40 miles (70 kilometers) thick beneath the world's tallest mountains. Beneath the crust lies the mantle, a semimolten layer of rock that flows in slow currents. At the earth's center is the core, composed of the outer and inner core. The outer core is about 1,400 miles (2,250 kilometers) thick and contains dense molten rocks. The inner core is an approximately 1,540-mile (2,480-kilometer) diameter ball of rock kept solid by intense pressure despite its high temperature (about 7,800 degrees F or 4,300 degrees C).

CHANGING ROCKS

Although rocks appear to be solid and stable, they actually are masses that are constantly changing and on the move. They metamorphose; they bend and fold under pressure; they travel as crustal plates on top of the under-lying mantle. Today, over a dozen crustal plates make up the earth's surface, although at different times in the past there have been both more and fewer that have broken apart or fused together over time. Scientists generally believe that the material composing the plates rises from ridges, seams in the earth where hot material pushes up from the mantle to the crust. Once it has sur-faced, the material cools, sinks, and moves outward from the ridges as if on a conveyer belt. The underlying mantle, with its constant, heat-driven flow, pro-vides the motion that conveys the crust from the ridges. The earth's core is the heat source, with temperatures estimated at 7,800 degrees F (4,300 degrees C). As heat radiates out from the core, it moves the surrounding mantle.

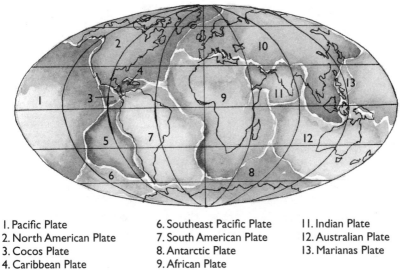

1. Pacific Plate
2. North American Plate
3. Cocos Plate
4. Caribbean Plate
5. Nazca Plate
6. Southeast Pacific Plate
7. South American Plate
8. Antarctic Plate
9. African Plate
10. Eurasian Plate
11. Indian Plate
12. Australian Plate
13. Marianas Plate

The earth's crust is broken into plates attached to an upper layer of the mantle. The plates fit together like pieces of a jigsaw puzzle. Scientists count the plates differently, resulting in varying and changing estimates of their number. The estimate illustrated here counts thirteen crustal plates.

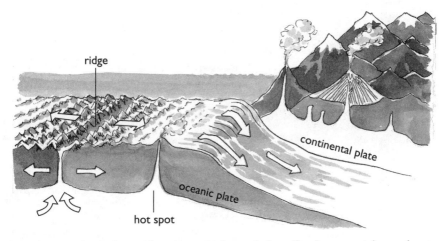

Crustal material rises from ridges, seams in the earth that allow hot material to push out and up from the mantle. Once the material has surfaced, it becomes part of a crustal plate that moves outward from the ridge in conveyer belt fashion. This drawing shows a ridge submerged under the ocean; the plate created at this submerged ridge is called an oceanic plate. Where the dense oceanic plate meets a lighter continental plate, the denser plate dives down beneath the continent.

CREATION AND DESTRUCTION OF PLATES

As crustal material rises from oceanic ridges, it pushes older crust before it; the farther the distance from a ridge, the older the crust. Although material has been created in this way for billions of years, it has not overwhelmed the earth's surface, and the earth does not grow in size. The reason is that crust recycles. After it spends a certain amount of time on the earth's surface, say several hundred million years, it is pulled back down toward the center of the earth, or subducted, at the far ends of the crustal conveyer belt.

To visualize the process of crustal creation and destruction, imagine yourself at one of the ridges where material is made. These ridges cross the globe in long lines known as rift zones, which look like the sutures on a baseball. One well-known and active rift zone, the Mid-Atlantic Ridge, is a series of smaller ridges that string together into a 36,000-mile (60,000-kilometer) long ridge that runs north and south through the middle of the Atlantic Ocean, up through Iceland and beyond. Material pushes up from the Mid-Atlantic Ridge

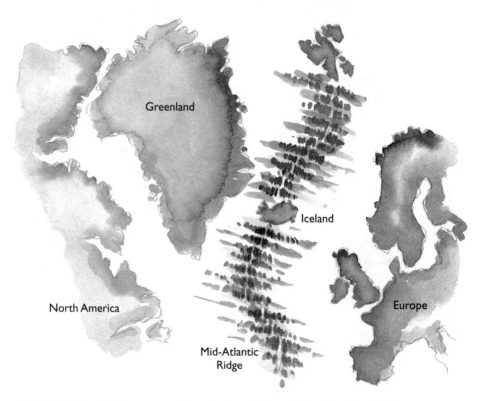

The Mid-Atlantic Ridge runs north-south through the middle of the Atlantic Ocean, up through Iceland, and down to the Antarctic Plate.

DISCOVER NATURE IN THE ROCKS

at the rate of a few inches or centimeters per year. As hot new rock encounters ocean water, great amounts of steam issue into the air. The rock cools quickly in the cold Atlantic, directly becoming a hardened layer of oceanic crust that travels on the slow conveyer belt both east and west from the ridge. In some places along the ridge, submarine volcanoes have built up on its crest. Such volcanoes were responsible for the creation of Iceland, where over many millions of years of activity they rose above sea level.

Imagine looking east and west along the crustal conveyer belt several thousand miles from the Mid-Atlantic Ridge to the continents of Europe and North America. The seafloor has been pushed outward from the ridge over time, and its spreading has pushed the continents apart with the crust. At other continental shores near other rift zones, however, the continents do not move farther apart. Instead, remarkably, the denser oceanic plate thrusts at an angle downward into a trench beneath the continental plate. Slowly, the crustal plate dives down toward the hot mantle, to be remelted by the earth's core heat. Once remelted to magma, it can either rise directly into overlying crust or remain in the mantle, oozing and flowing, awaiting later recycling.

All of this heating and pushing affects the continental crust as well. Parts of the crust may fold, melt, or break along faults. The affected rocks give clues to the dynamic interactions of the plates.

ROCK TYPES

Three types of rocks are found on earth: igneous, sedimentary, and metamorphic. Rocks are grouped by type according to the different earth processes that make them.

Igneous Rocks. Igneous means "of fire." Most igneous rocks are masses of minerals that crystallize out of burning-hot liquids found deep in the earth. Igneous rocks are found as both underground, plutonic rocks (named for Pluto, Greek god of the underworld) and aboveground, volcanic rocks (named for Vulcan, Roman god of fire and metalworking). At various points along the rifting and conveyer belt system, igneous rocks are formed, crystallizing as masses of minerals when hot magmas cool. The change from liquid to solid can occur in magma that erupts from midoceanic ridges and suddenly encounters cold seawater. The change can also occur in the hot oozing magma that remelts and rises from the trenches into the higher, cooler crust. Hot magma also turns solid as it is spewed into the air from the cone of a volcano that has formed over the trenches at the continental plates.

The color and appearance of an igneous rock depend on which minerals crystallize from a magma and how large their crystals grow. If a magma is rich in silica, it tends to give rise to light-colored igneous rocks with light-colored minerals such as quartz, alkali feldspars, and muscovite mica. These rocks contain significant amounts of potassium, sodium, and aluminum in the feldspar minerals orthoclase, albite, oligoclase, and andesine, as well as in the mica muscovite. Rocks that contain less silica may be rich in dark-colored ferromagnesian minerals (minerals with significant amounts of iron and magnesium), such as hornblende, augite, biotite, magnetite, and olivine, but they do not contain silica-rich quartz. The silica-poor rocks also tend to have calcium-rich feldspars (such as labradorite), rather than alkali feldspars. If a magma cools slowly below the surface of the earth, mineral grains can have much time and space to grow large, as in granites and gabbros. If a magma quenches quickly, as it does when it hits seawater or blasts as lava from a volcano directly into the air, mineral grains can be small, even microscopic, as in basalt or rhyolite. The cooling may be so quick that no minerals crystallize; the result is volcanic glass, or obsidian. Some common igneous rocks are described below; check a good reference, such as those listed at the end of this chapter, to read further about certain igneous rocks.

Granite: Granite is a pink- or gray-colored plutonic rock that has medium to large mineral grains. It is rich in silica, potassium, and sodium and thereby rich in quartz and alkali feldspars. It has smaller amounts of micas and hornblende. In mountainous areas, granite forms domes, crags, spires, and castle shapes. The name granite is also used in a collective sense for several light-colored rocks (with one-third or less dark minerals by volume), including granite proper, made of the minerals quartz, feldspar, and mica.

Gabbro: Gabbro is another rock that forms underground. It, too, is coarse grained, with crystals large enough to be seen easily without the help of a hand lens or microscope. Gabbro crystallizes slowly, deep within the earth, so its crystals have time to grow large. Composed of darker minerals than granite, gabbro has the main (essential) minerals calcium-rich plagioclase feldspar, pyroxene, amphibole, and olivine.

Basalt: Basalt is another common igneous rock, although strikingly different from granite and gabbro. It crystallizes when magmas with compositions similar to those that form gabbro erupt on the earth's surface. Like gabbro, basalt is dark in color, made of the common minerals feldspar, pyroxene, apatite, and magnetite. The crystals in basalt are so small and fine grained, however, that they are hard to see even with a hand lens.

Rhyolite: Rhyolite is another volcanic rock that is light in color like granite. Rhyolite forms when magmas with granitelike compositions push to the earth's surface. Rhyolite tends to be fine grained because of rapid cooling aboveground,

four common igneous rocks

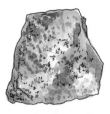

Granite is a pink or gray plutonic rock with medium to large mineral grains.

Domes, crags, spires, and castle shapes form in areas where large bodies of granite have been exposed by erosion. Half Dome in Yosemite National Park, California, is a granitic dome.

Gabbro is another plutonic rock with dark-colored minerals large enough to be visible without using a hand lens or microscope.

Rhyolite, a fine-grained volcanic rock, should be examined for flow lines, created when the magma is still hot and moving.

Basalt, a common igneous rock popularly known as lava, often forms in thick flows that cool and solidify into layers of rock broken into columns by vertical joints. Basalt columns like these in Devil's Postpile National Monument, California, can be seen in many areas of past volcanic activity.

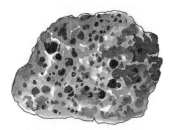

Samples of basalt may contain numerous cavities that formed when trapped gases escaped from the cooling magma.

and it can be confused sometimes with sandstones and other fine-grained sedimentary rocks. Look closely for indications of flow in rhyolites, such as mineral grains that are stretched out flat into stripes, or flow lines. The crystals elongated in a magma that was probably still hot and flowing.

Sedimentary Rocks. Sedimentary means "a settling." Sedimentary rocks are made of particles that have been moved by wind and water and have come to rest in rivers, lakes, ponds, seas, sand dunes, deltas, and deserts. Over time, the particles have been cemented together. The particles, or sediments, that compose sedimentary rocks can be of all sizes, from submicroscopic to larger than a house, and include pebbles, sand, pieces of shell, microscopic mineral grains, silt, mud, and clay. The sediments may have originally erupted from a volcano or may be pieces of plutonic or older sedimentary rocks. Sedimentary rocks are also the rocks most likely to hold fossils, the remains of plants and animals that were buried as the sediments were deposited.

Sedimentary rocks are explored further in chapter 4; a few common types include the following:

Sandstone: Sandstone is composed of generally rounded particles no larger than .08 inch (2 millimeters) in diameter. The particles are often held together by a finer-grained sedimentary cement. Sandstone varies widely in color and hardness, depending on the amount and type of cement and the type and color of grain material. Quartz is usually the main mineral in sandstone. Look for large sandstone blocks in the walls of older buildings.

Shale: Shale or mudstone is finer grained than sandstone, made of microscopic particles of silt and clay that have been compacted into thin, hard layers. Shale looks light to dark gray, depending on the sediments that compose it. A knife blade will easily scratch a shale, which will also easily split along its horizontal layers much as a mineral splits along cleavage planes. Certain shales, known as oil shales, contain dark coal-like material that in some cases has been distilled into oil.

Conglomerate: Conglomerate is a coarse-grained sedimentary rock with rounded particles of many sizes ranging from pebbles, .08 to 2.5 inches (2 to 64 millimeters) in diameter, to boulders greater than 10 feet (3 meters) in diameter. The particles are usually surrounded by finer-grained material called the matrix. The entire mix of particles and matrix is held together by silica- or calcite-rich cement. Color and hardness vary greatly depending on the type of rock particles that make up the conglomerate; these may be minerals or pieces of igneous, sedimentary, or metamorphic rocks. As in sandstones, conglomerates are only as strong as their cement.

three common sedimentary rocks

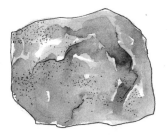

Sandstone is made of sand particles, often held together by sedimentary cement. Sandstone may be soft or hard depending on the composition of the cement.

Thick layers of sandstone can weather into landforms with many colors and shapes, especially in arid regions where the layers are well exposed. Formations like these can be seen in desert regions of Africa and the southwestern United States.

Shale consists of microscopic particles of silt and clay compacted into thin, hard layers parallel to sedimentary bedding. Shale tends to split along these layers.

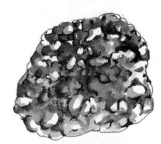

Conglomerate has rounded particles that can range in size from pebbles to boulders held in a finer-grained material called the matrix.

Limestone: Limestone is a dense, fine-grained rock that is usually white, light or dark gray, or black. The particles making up most limestones are so fine that they can be viewed only through a microscope. The particles can be microscopic fossils, tiny broken shell fragments, pieces of crystals of the mineral calcite, or fragments of other limestones. Limestones usually occur in layers, called beds, that range in thickness from a few inches or centimeters to more than 100 feet (30 meters) thick. Crushed limestone is an important ingredient of cement, mortar, and some concretes.

Limestone is usually so dense that it can be studied well only under a microscope.

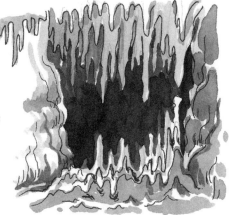

Some limestones are laced with networks of underground channels and caves, where dripping water deposits stalactites from cave ceilings and stalagmites from cave floors.

Often no striking textural patterns can be seen in limestones unless they contain fossils, as in this shelly limestone.

Coal: Coal is a dense, sometimes glassy sedimentary rock derived from decayed and compressed organic (plant and animal) matter. Its structure varies depending on how much the original organic matter has been altered by decay and compression: Peat is the spongy product of partly decomposed plant remains; lignite has an obvious woody structure; bituminous coal is harder, often thinly layered, with some fossil plant matter visible through a

the formation of coal

vegetation	Masses of vegetation before decomposition.	Masses of vegetation settle in areas of poor drainage, such as swamps and low-lying forests.
peat	Some roots and other remains are still visible.	The rotting vegetation has been compacted, yielding peat. Peat can be cut into blocks, dried, and used for fuel.
lignite ("brown coal")	Crumbly brown substance with some plant fragments still visible.	Lignite is peat that is further compacted such that more moisture is driven out.
bituminous coal	Hard and brittle substance. Dirty with a charcoal-like powder.	The application of more pressure results in bituminous coal, which is harder, blacker, and drier than lignite.
anthracite	The hardest coal. Clean to the touch. Produces the most heat and the least smoke.	Buried vegetation that has undergone the greatest pressures yields anthracite coal, a hard, black shiny coal with 96 percent carbon.

Coal is made when dead plants are buried and compacted. Increased burial pressure on the plants results in a higher carbon content and greater fuel value.

hand lens; and anthracite coal is a high-grade, jet black, massive coal that fractures in conchoidal shapes. Anthracite coal is the gem-quality coal called jet. Coal beds or seams often occur in thin layers within other sedimentary rocks.

Metamorphic Rocks. The third group, metamorphic, takes its name from the verb *metamorphose,* which means "to change form." Metamorphic rocks are altered igneous, sedimentary, or older metamorphic rocks, products of high pressures, high temperatures, and chemical activity. Changes can be small, as when a layer of shale is squeezed under the weight of overlying sediment just enough to be compressed into slate, or great, as when the igneous rock granite partially remelts under heat and pressure to form a banded metamorphic rock known as gneiss. As a rock is altered or metamorphosed, its minerals change their shapes and chemical makeups. They line up differently and may squeeze into fantastic patterns.

Metamorphism by Heat. Crustal temperatures are coolest near the surface of the earth. Heat radiates from the core of the earth, and rock material beneath the crust is kept molten by the heat. The mantle or rising magma bodies heat crustal rock enough to cause partial remelting in a sort of baked zone. In some places, the heat is great enough to rearrange molecules within minerals, forming new metamorphic minerals. The list of minerals that are likely to be found in a zone metamorphosed by heat is fairly long, and the minerals range from common to obscure. They include the micas biotite, muscovite, and phlogopite; the feldspars albite and orthoclase; and chlorite, hornblende, magnetite, and quartz. Rocks formed by heat metamorphism include marble from former limestone, hornfels (a metamorphic rock that is usually dark and dense, has a dull luster, and is prone to conchoidal fracture) from former mudstone, and metaquartzite from quartz-rich sandstone.

The places in the crust where heat metamorphism is likely to occur are beneath volcanoes, deep in subduction zones where crustal plates remelt, and deep in the crust near the heat of the mantle.

Metamorphism by Pressure. As crustal plates move over the surface of the earth, pushed by the rifting of new material, they collide and grind together in other places. These areas of collision and grinding are subject to much pressure, as can occur anywhere two objects push together. Sometimes the pressure between plates is released suddenly, causing earthquakes. In other instances, pushing together of the plates causes a massive piling up of crust, building spectacular mountain ranges. An example is the Alpine-Himalayan mountain belt in Asia, where Mount Everest and other high peaks

As two plates carrying land masses collide, the crust crumples and piles up, building mountains. In the Himalayan Mountains, crustal material has piled up to a thickness of 42 miles (70 kilometers), the thickest crust on earth.

result from two large crustal plates pushing together, neither plate being able to dive beneath the other into a trench; instead, the colliding plates have climbed skyward. The crustal material in the Himalayas is thicker than anywhere else on the earth's surface. In an area of such great pressure, rocks bend, fold, and break.

High pressures allow molecules in individual crystals to move about as they do when metamorphosed by heat. Among the many minerals formed when others are subjected to pressure are the micas biotite, muscovite, and phlogopite; the feldspars albite, andesine, microcline, oligoclase, and orthoclase; as well as calcite, chlorite, corundum, kyanite, magnetite, and quartz.

Metamorphism by Water. A rock can be metamorphosed by water that is superheated (540 to 900 degrees F or 300 to 500 degrees C) and mineral rich. Usually such extremely hot, mineral-laden water has been heated by the very high temperatures within a magma still in the process of crystallizing. The superheated fluids then work through surrounding rock, changing its structure or mineral composition by adding or removing minerals. Such metamorphism is known as hydrothermal metamorphism. Biotite, calcite, chlorite, galena, hematite, magnetite, pyrite, quartz, and tourmaline are among the minerals common in hydrothermal metamorphic rocks. Native elements such as gold, silver, copper, and lead, deposited in cavities and fissures by hot solutions, are often associated with hydrothermally altered rocks.

Metamorphic rocks will not be discussed in great detail in this book, but a few important types are described below. For more photographs and

five common metamorphic rocks

Slate is metamorphosed shale and is easily split into thin sheets along parallel planes. Shiny flakes of mica may be visible on sheet surfaces.

Metaquartzite, an altered quartz-rich sandstone with a hardness around 7, has an uneven, often conchoidal fracture.

Schist is medium to coarse grained with distinct parallel mineral alignment from metamorphism by heat and pressure.

The intense folding displayed in layers of granular minerals in gneisses takes place deep in the earth's crust.

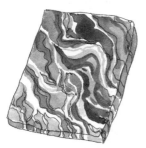

Pure marble, composed of only calcite or dolomite, is generally pure white. Other minerals act as coloring agents, adding spots or veinlike patterns known as marbling.

Marble, with a hardness of 3, can easily be scratched with a knife blade. For ages, sculptors have carved statues and ornaments of marble.

explanations, consult a thorough field guide (see "To Read" section at the end of this chapter).

Slate: Slate is a dense, thin-sheeted rock that readily splits along parallel planes. It results from the metamorphism of shale by the combined work of heat and pressure. The thin sheets may contain shiny bits of mica or scattered larger crystals such as garnet, a hard, cubic, often deep red to purple mineral rich in aluminum and silica. Slate is a popular rock for use as roofing material, flagstone, and blackboards.

Schist: Schist is a medium- to coarse-grained rock with obvious parallel lines of minerals. Schists may be formed from sedimentary, volcanic, or other metamorphic rocks that undergo combined heat and pressure. Just how hot a rock has been during metamorphism can be told from certain minerals found in it, called index minerals. Chlorite, a green platy mineral, is one mineral found in schists that have metamorphosed at temperatures of 300 to 500 degrees F (150 to 250 degrees C); garnets are found in rocks that formed at 500 to 850 degrees F (250 to 450 degrees C); kyanite, a blue mineral that grows in blades, is found in schists that metamorphosed at 850 to 1,300 degrees F (450 to 700 degrees C). When searching for schists, look for wavy and folded lines of minerals on fresh surfaces of silver-white rocks or on older brown and yellow surfaces.

Gneisses: Gneisses are more strikingly banded than schists. They too are medium- to coarse-grained rocks with minerals in obvious lines, but the lines are so prominent as to be layers. Gneisses have narrow bands of quartz and feldspar alternating with darker minerals such as micas and hornblendes. They form at great pressures and temperatures and have the same index minerals as schists. The most common parent rocks for gneisses are igneous plutonic rocks such as granite and gabbro; sedimentary rocks such as shale, sandstone, and conglomerate; and lower-grade metamorphic rocks such as slate, schist, and marble.

Marble: Marble is a soft to hard, fine- to medium-grained rock typically composed of calcite and a related mineral, dolomite. Marble is white when pure, but scattered minerals throughout can give it different colors, such as gray, black, green, red, or yellow to brown. Marble forms when limestone or layers of dolomite are heated by nearby hot magma or are subjected to combined heat and pressure. The rock is commonly quarried for use in statues and buildings.

Metaquartzite: Metaquartzite is a metamorphosed, quartz-rich sandstone. Under heat and pressure, the original quartz cement in the softer sandstone recrystallizes, and outlines of the parent quartz grains are not detectable. Metaquartzite is tough and hard, with an uneven conchoidal fracture. It can range from white through light and dark gray to pink and brown.

TO DO

IDENTIFYING ROCKS
What you will need
hand lens

copper penny

pocketknife

geology field guide

notebook

Rocks can be described in terms of a handful of properties that can be observed in the field, home, or laboratory.

You can identify rocks anywhere you travel outside—to the beach, hills, empty lots, or downtown, where some buildings are made of granite, sandstone, metaquartzite, or marble. Look closely at the rocks you see. Are they arranged in layers in the face of a cliff? Sketch them. Do you see pebbles, boulders, or sand grains? Fossils and shells? If so, what type of rock is it? Do you see layers and lines of minerals swirling through very hard rock? You may be looking at a schist or gneiss. Consult your field guide or sketch the rocks for later identification from your notes and sketches.

Test the rock with your fingernail. Can you scratch it? If so, you may have found a sandstone or a very soft limestone called chalk. Apply the Mohs scale of hardness for minerals from chapter 1 to the rocks, too. A copper penny will scratch some limestones; a pocketknife will scratch shale and harder marbles. Note the rock's hardness in your notebook.

Which rocks do you find occurring together? Which have many colors and textures? Which are found in buildings and walls? Some walls and buildings are made of a type of concrete cast into the shapes of stones. They can look very real, but can you tell which are not?

Explanation: Each time you study them, the rocks will tell you more. As with any part of nature, the more familiar you become with them, the more you will learn.

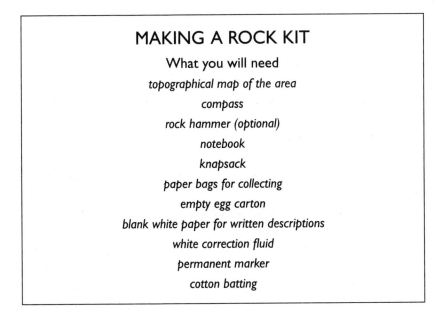

You can make a collection of the sorted pieces of rock you find on your field trips.

Do not collect on private or government-owned property without first getting permission from the landowners or stewards. Also, observe basic safety measures when breaking rocks with a hammer or climbing and walking around; it helps to wear good field boots, safety glasses, and sun protection. Keep track of your location using a map and compass.

Choose specimens that are as unweathered as possible, and select or break off pieces with your rock hammer that are large enough to show characterizing features but small enough to be carried easily in your knapsack. Write notes in your field notebook regarding where you collected it, what the area looked like, what rocks you suspect were present, and how soft or hard they were. Then bag your specimens and make legible notes on the bags. Give the rock a number, and write that number on the bag and in your notebook.

When you get them home, sort your rocks according to the information in your field notes. Dab each specimen with a bit of white correction fluid. When that has dried, mark the number on each rock that corresponds to your notebook entry. Write explanations to tape inside the lid of the empty egg carton, and place your specimens into the corresponding egg pockets.

You may decide to have several rock kits, one for plutonic igneous rocks, one for volcanic igneous rocks, one for fine-grained sedimentary rocks, and so on. Keep the specimens in place with pieces of cotton batting and the cartons secured with rubber bands when storing the kits. Then any time you want to study your collection or refer to your field notes, your specimens will be handy.

Explanation: You may not be sure you have positively identified a rock when you collect it, but your field notes and later observations of your rock kit will tell you much about what type of rock it is, which minerals it contains, and how it formed. Remember that observations are more important than names!

EDIBLE "ROCKS"

What you will need

various candies and cookies

dinner plates

notebook

pen

field geology guide

This edible "rock" experiment is best shared with friends.

Place each type of candy and cookie on a separate plate on a table. You may have, for example, brownies, chocolate chip cookies, malted milk balls, hard toffee, Rice Krispies treats, milk chocolate bars, and peanut butter cups, each on a different plate. Describe each type of sweet as you would a rock: Does it have layers? Does it have conchoidal fracture? What are the particle sizes? Is it hard or soft? If you have asked friends or family members to help you with this exercise, give them pen and paper and ask them to record their impressions of each type. Use the field guide to associate the samples with real rock types.

Your conclusions might be something like this:

Hard toffee has conchoidal fracture like obsidian.

Chocolate chip cookies have scattered larger particles in a fine-grained mass, like garnet schist.

Rice Krispies treats have large pieces cemented together, like conglomerate.

You have many choices while conducting your experiment. Be creative! Then eat the "rocks."

Explanation: In identifying rocks, all our senses come into play. An oil shale not only looks but smells oily, with its layer of dark organic matter. The sedimentary particles in sandstone are coarser than the finer-grained sedimentary particles in mudstone. Try "tasting" a mudstone to test how it feels on the teeth and tongue. Learning to use taste, touch, and smell as well as sight helps in identifying rocks.

COOKING UP A CONGLOMERATE

What you will need

recipe for Rice Krispies treats

ingredients for treats

rice puff cereal

wheat puff cereal

cake pan

large saucepan

mixing bowls and spoons

measuring spoons and cups

field rock identification guide

You can bake your own conglomerate, which can be used in the experiment above.

Follow the Rice Krispies treats recipe directions, but use ⅓ Rice Krispies, ⅓ wheat puffs, and ⅓ rice puffs instead of all Rice Krispies. Once you have made the conglomeratic mixture, spread it into the baking pan. After you have cooled the treats, note the appearance of the particles in size, shape, and color. Then taste your samples; you may discover something else worth noting.

Explanation: Conglomerate is a sedimentary rock composed of various-sized rock particles cemented together. The various-sized cereal pieces in your concoction simulate rock particles in a conglomerate.

Usually the cementing of rock particles occurs slowly over long periods of time. In this experiment, consolidation occurs in hours rather than years.

Breccia is a rock type that differs from conglomerate only in that its particles are angular rather than round. If you substitute jagged pieces of nuts and dried fruits for puffed rice and wheat, you are using angular particles and composing a mock breccia.

TO THINK ABOUT

Geologic Time. In 1788, in Berwickshire, Scotland, a gentleman farmer and physician named James Hutton stood on Siccar Point, a rock promontory near the ocean. The promontory, with its tilted layers of sandstone overlain by horizontal layers of sandstone, had fascinated him for some time. Although Hutton did not know which forces had raised the land, he deduced that the older sandstones had settled in place before the younger. Both in turn had been pushed up and uncovered by erosive forces. Before the younger rocks were deposited, the older rocks had been worn down over many years by the effects of wind and water. Later, the effects of wind and ocean waves wore down the younger rocks.

Hutton postulated that the rocks were moving through a cycle that must continuously repeat. His ideas were the basis for the Principle of Uniformitarianism, a rule that states that the same forces at work in and on the earth today have been at work throughout its history. Hutton wrote that the earth's cycles have "no vestige of a beginning, no prospect of an end."

His principle opened the door to modern geologic research. Geologists now examine ancient rocks knowing they formed mostly gradually, in the same manner similar rocks form in various environments today. In applying the Principle of Uniformitarianism, however, geologists have also learned that the earth is very old. The tilted sandstones observed by Hutton were later estimated by modern methods to be 450 million years old; the horizontal sandstones were estimated at 370 million years old. Their deposition took time as well: Great amounts of time were needed for the sediments to settle; great amounts of time were needed for their consolidation and cementation.

Our everyday notion of time has to expand when we study rocks. Probably the best way to grasp the concept of geologic time is to imagine all the earth's history passing in a single year. If 4.6 billion years were compressed into twelve months, the oldest rocks would date from approximately mid-March. The first life, ancient sea organisms, appeared in May. Many months passed until plants and animals emerge in late November. Dinosaurs did not dominate the earth until mid-December, disappearing approximately the day after Christmas. Early humans appeared in the evening of December 31, and the most recent ice ages ended just before midnight that night. Then, according to Don Eicher's book *Geologic Time*:

Rome ruled the Western world for 5 seconds, from 11:59:45 to 11:59:50. Columbus discovered America 3 seconds before midnight, and the science of geology was born with the writings of James Hutton just slightly more than one second before the end of our eventful year of years.

Such vastness of time when truly contemplated brings an element of awe to the study of geologic processes.

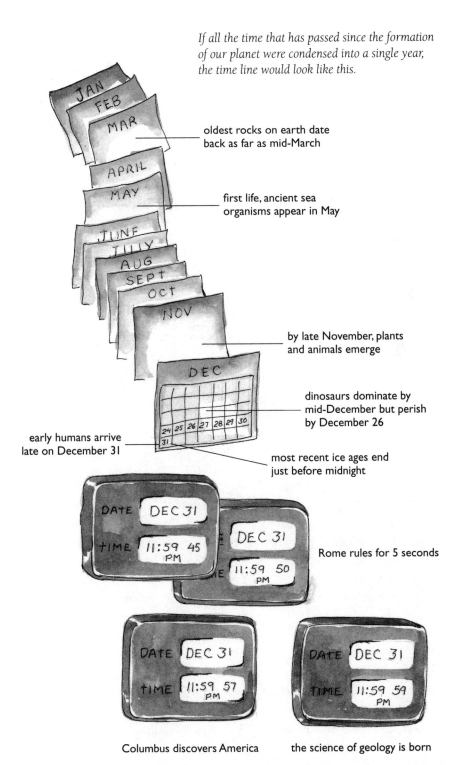

If all the time that has passed since the formation of our planet were condensed into a single year, the time line would look like this.

oldest rocks on earth date back as far as mid-March

first life, ancient sea organisms appear in May

by late November, plants and animals emerge

dinosaurs dominate by mid-December but perish by December 26

early humans arrive late on December 31

most recent ice ages end just before midnight

DATE DEC 31
TIME 11:59 45 PM

DEC 31
11:59 50 PM

Rome rules for 5 seconds

DATE DEC 31
TIME 11:59 57 PM

Columbus discovers America

DATE DEC 31
TIME 11:59 59 PM

the science of geology is born

the rock cycle

Weathering can break down rocks carrying particles to be deposited as sediment.

Sedimentary rocks are formed as layers of sediment are compacted over time.

Metamorphic rocks are created when sedimentary or igneous rocks are subjected to great heat and pressure.

With further heating, metamorphic rocks melt, becoming molten magma.

Igneous extrusive rocks (volcanic) form when volcanic material erupts and cools at the surface.

Igneous intrusive rocks (plutonic) form deep within the earth from molten magma. They may be exposed by weathering.

Magma can be forced to the surface by volcanic activity.

The Rock Cycle. As Dr. James Hutton observed, the geologic processes we observe today have been occurring for all time and will continue to occur. Time and rock form a cycle: Not only does crustal rock recycle into trenches to be remelted and re-created as new crust, but rocks undergo a cycle of weathering, compaction, metamorphism, surfacing, intruding, and extruding that, although slow, has a definite endless quality. Think of any rock in terms of its place in the rock cycle. Is it undergoing weathering, soon to be transported in pieces as sediment? Was it recently extruded after millennia of metamorphism underground? As we stand on familiar ground, our place on the crust, where are we in the rock cycle?

TO READ

Eicher, D. C. *Geologic Time.* Englewood Cliffs, NJ: Prentice Hall, 1976. This book tells about the phenomenon of vast time.

Parker, Steve. *Rocks and Minerals.* New York: Dorling Kindersley, 1993. This

Eyewitness Explorers book contains many informative color photographs of various rocks.

Skinner, Brian J. *The Dynamic Earth: An Introduction to Physical Geology.* New York: Wiley, 1992. The diagrams and photographs in this book are highly recommended.

TO WATCH

The Voyage of the Lee. United States Geological Survey, 1985. This film shows the *Lee,* a United States Geological Survey ship, sampling rocks on the floor of the Pacific Ocean.

CHAPTER 3

Volcanoes: Mountains of Hot Rock

Spectacular mountain ranges like the Himalayas can form when crustal plates collide and grind together. Some of our best-known mountains, however, originated altogether differently—as volcanoes. Kilauea in Hawaii, Mount Katmai in Alaska, and Mount Rainier in Washington State are just a few volcanic mountains. Each formed when hot rock, or magma, welled up high enough to reach the surface of the earth.

TYPES OF ERUPTIONS

Each volcanic eruption is different. The world has as many kinds of eruptions as it has volcanoes, and any single volcano may act differently with each outburst. Geologists have identified six general types of volcanic eruptions—Hawaiian, Strombolian, Vulcanian, Vesuvian, Plinian, and Peléean—chiefly named for classic volcanic eruptions that occurred many years ago. The type of eruption that occurs at a volcano depends on the temperature and composition of the magma. The more silica in the melt, the thicker and more viscous (sticky and resistant to flow) the magma.

Hawaiian eruptions tend to be quiet outpourings of runny lava that flow easily downhill. Over the years, lava has erupted frequently from Mauna Loa, the world's largest active volcano, on the island of Hawaii. During the eruptions, lava often flows toward the port town of Hilo, about 25 (40 kilometers) miles away. In one eruption in 1935, magma burst from high up the volcano and flowed downhill to threaten the town, so geologists asked the U.S. Air Force to attack the lava. Ten bombers carrying 600-pound (270-kilogram)

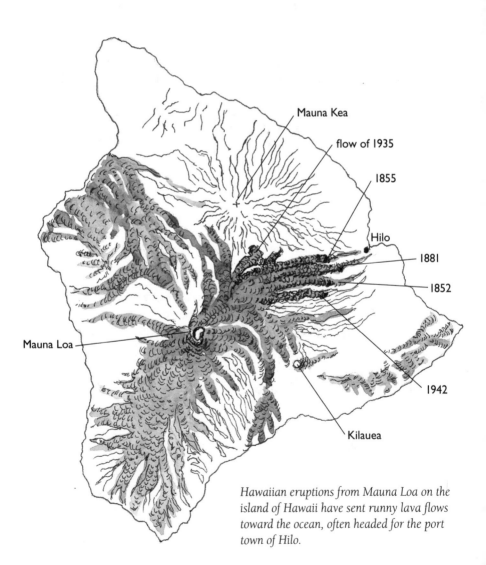

Hawaiian eruptions from Mauna Loa on the island of Hawaii have sent runny lava flows toward the ocean, often headed for the port town of Hilo.

DISCOVER NATURE IN THE ROCKS

When lava spouts high into the air and is caught by the wind, it elongates into light gold glassy strands called "Pele's hair."

explosives flew two raids that blasted the flow far up the mountain's flanks. New runny flows broke off to the sides and poured away from Hilo. Soon the main flow stopped altogether as the runny lavas spread off and away.

In some Hawaiian eruptions, fountains of liquid rock fly into the air. If caught by the wind, the shooting lava is drawn out into glassy strands called "Pele's hair," named for Pele, Hawaiian goddess of fire.

Strombolian eruptions, noisier and more violent than Hawaiian eruptions, are named for the volcano Stromboli, on a small island off the coast of Italy. Stromboli has been erupting almost continuously for centuries, lighting up the night and drawing the attention of boatloads of tourists. The frequent eruptions send fragments of the lava short distances into the air to trace glowing paths, twists, and turns before falling to rest near the vent of the volcano or bouncing and clattering down its ash-covered slopes.

Vulcanian eruptions, in which the magma is still thicker, throw larger pieces of lava greater distances than Strombolian and can destroy parts of the volcano. Such eruptions are named for Vulcano, a volcanic island off the shore of Sicily and southwest of Stromboli. Vulcano in turn takes its name from the Roman god of fire, Vulcan. In Vulcanian eruptions, red-hot blocks of rock may travel over a mile, and gas and fine ash shoot up in a plume several miles high that rolls in tight curls, followed by a knobby, cauliflower-shaped cloud.

Vesuvian eruptions are even more explosive, typically destroying huge portions of the cone. They blow out ash and rock for many hours, as in the

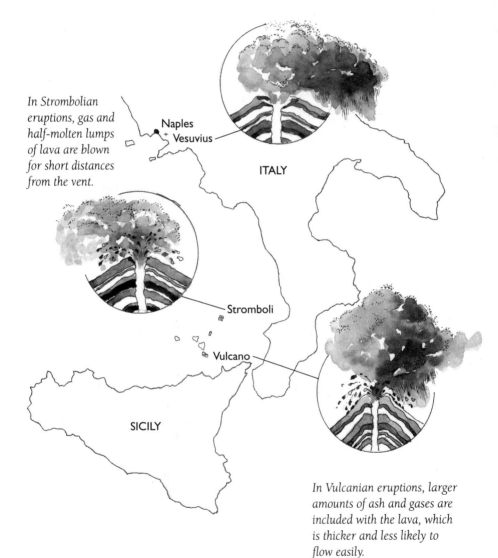

In Vesuvian eruptions, plumes of gas and ash shoot high into the atmosphere, and large parts of the volcano are blown away.

In Strombolian eruptions, gas and half-molten lumps of lava are blown for short distances from the vent.

Naples

Vesuvius

ITALY

Stromboli

Vulcano

SICILY

In Vulcanian eruptions, larger amounts of ash and gases are included with the lava, which is thicker and less likely to flow easily.

great eruption of the Italian volcano Mount Vesuvius. In Vesuvian eruptions, rocks that fly from the vent are not old, shattered pieces of the mountain like Strombolian or Vulcanian bombs. Until 79 A.D., Vesuvius had been inactive, with no records of eruptions. Then, on the morning of August 24, a large mushroom cloud grew thousands of yards high over the volcano. Volcanic ash and pumice rained down on the fields and homes surrounding the mountain. The eruption continued through the night, lighting the sky with the glow of the eruption and fires set by falling ash. The greatest blast was yet to come, and those people who had not evacuated from the area were in mortal danger.

The sky never brightened the next day, because enough ash clouded the air to darken the sun. Soon a great blast of gas blew off the mountaintop, and a heavier fall of ash continued for hours. When it stopped, dozens of square miles of countryside had been buried. The town of Pompeii had been overwhelmed by ash; Herculaneum, on the far side of the mountain, had been covered in a rapid flow of ash and pumice turned to mud by hard rains that fell from the great cloud over Vesuvius.

The shape of Mount Vesuvius changed dramatically during the volcanic eruption in 79 A.D. Large parts of the volcano, which had been cone shaped and symmetrical, collapsed or were blown away. A dish-shaped mountain was left behind after the eruption.

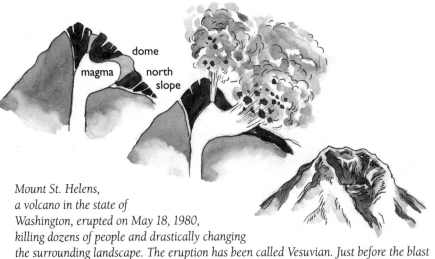

*Mount St. Helens,
a volcano in the state of
Washington, erupted on May 18, 1980,
killing dozens of people and drastically changing
the surrounding landscape. The eruption has been called Vesuvian. Just before the blast
occurred, a growing bulge became apparent on the north slope of the mountain. On the
day of the eruption, the north face of the mountain shattered. Mount St.Helens lost almost
1 cubic mile of material from its summit, changing from a mountain with an elevation of
over 9,600 feet (2,900 meters) to less than 8,400 feet (2,500 meters).*

Plinian eruptions, named for a man called Pliny the Younger, who witnessed the Vesuvius eruption, are violent and forceful like Vesuvius's final blasts. Large parts of the volcano blow apart or collapse. An example of a Plinian eruption was demonstrated by a volcano on the island of Krakatoa, between Java and Sumatra, which blew up in the nineteenth century in a fiery glory that outstripped even Vesuvius. In a cluster of tiny islands on a well-traveled sea lane, Krakatoa was uninhabited and rarely visited, a place of tranquil beauty. Ships' records suggest that the volcano had stayed quiet for more than two hundred years.

In May 1883, after nearly a decade of increased earth shaking in the area, Krakatoa came to life. Steam and ash were emitted for many weeks, showering ash on villages up to 300 miles (500 kilometers) distant. Three months of eruptions followed from several cones on the cluster of islands. Inhabitants on nearby shores learned to live with ground shaking until August 26 and 27, when massive explosions shook the world. Great blasts from Krakatoa woke sleeping people 2,000 miles (3,000 kilometers) away; gunfire-type cracks traveled 3,000 miles (5,000 kilometers), the farthest distance sound has carried and been heard without the help of special instruments. Great waves, called tsunamis, swept the neighboring coasts, washing away three hundred towns and thirty-six thousand people. Ash covered the decks of sailing ships that floundered in darkness. Visibility was so obscured that no one could tell what was happening on Krakatoa.

After one hundred days of Plinian eruptions and a final four days of violent explosions that can only be called Krakatoan, the volcano gave a last gasp and returned to silence. In the heavy outbursts, parts of the existing islands, including half of Krakatoa Island, had been blown away. Nothing of such lasting power has been seen on earth since.

Peléean eruptions, quite different from Vesuvian, Plinian, or Krakatoan, spew out glowing, hot clouds of solid fragments that sweep down volcanoes on a rush of heated gases. These glowing clouds, or *nuée ardentes*, were first described after the St. Pierre disaster in 1902 on the Caribbean island Martinique. Near the town of St. Pierre, volcanic Mount Pelée made a series of small sputters and explosions that threw ash and hot rock into the air. The mountain had erupted before, but not in fifty years. As the volcanic activity increased, so did the panic of the people in the nearby town of St. Pierre. Many decided to evacuate, but some stayed in hopes that the volcano would quiet down again.

On May 8, the mountain roared and cracked, and a *nuée ardente* shot skyward, then swept swiftly toward St. Pierre. A very thick lava had plugged Mount Pelée, forcing gas-rich lava to escape out the side of the volcano in a

Nuée ardentes (*glowing clouds*) *blast out of volcanic vents and ride heated gases swiftly down mountainsides.*

violent surge. The fiery cloud traveled more than 100 miles (180 kilometers) an hour, carried on a blast of fiercely hot gas that engulfed St. Pierre and left the town in flames, with all but two townspeople dead.

No real-life volcanic eruption is purely one type or another. One phase of a single eruption may be Hawaiian, for instance, and a later phase may be Vulcanian. The rock types deep within the volcano determine in part how it will erupt. In Hawaiian volcanoes, the thin, runny lavas, composed chiefly of low-silica basalt, flow out because they are so hot. Hotter rocks flow easier and faster, the way honey and syrup spread more quickly when warm. Basalt melts at temperatures of about 2,000 degrees F (1,000 degrees C); other rocks melt at much cooler temperatures. Granite melts at about 1,000 degrees F (500 degrees C), and its cooler, thicker texture forces gases to build up pressure before they can be released. At Mount Pelée, the thick lava plugging the vent was made of a rock close in mineral makeup to granite.

Sometimes, two magmas may be the same thickness, but one has more gases trapped inside. Even a basaltic lava with high gas content can erupt with a bang if gases have built up enough pressure before their release.

WHERE PLATES MEET

The rock type found within a volcano depends on where it is on the earth's crustal plates. No volcanoes are found anywhere on the entire impressive length of the Alpine-Himalayan belt, because volcanoes are not found where two continental plates have collided and pushed up. Instead, volcanoes often form when an oceanic plate bumps into a continental plate. There, the heavier, thinner crust of the seafloor dives beneath the continent, slides under it, and melts as the oceanic plate absorbs heat from the mantle. The dark rocks of oceanic plates are basalt, and as they melt and rise back to the earth's surface, they melt rocks from the continental crust as well. Depending on how much of the continental crust melts, different kinds of magmas result. If enough continental, or granitic, crust melts, the magma within a volcano will be closer to granite in composition.

Some rock may rise only partway and cool slowly to form huge batholiths (Greek for "deep rocks"), but melted material that rises as far as the surface will erupt as lava and volcanic ash. At one time, the Sierra Nevada in California had many active volcanoes that formed as the Pacific Plate slid beneath the North American Plate. Huge batholiths of granite and other rock formed deep in the heart of the mountains. Over time, the volcanoes became inactive and were stripped away by erosion during later uplift. Much of the granite in the batholiths remains, however, and can be seen in such places as Yosemite Valley

Magma that rises only partway to the surface cools slowly. Batholiths, huge bodies of magma that cooled deep in the earth, are exposed in Yosemite Valley, California, following millions of years of uplift and erosion that stripped off the overlying volcanic rock.

and Hetch Hetchy. The mountains of the Sierra are part of a chain that extends beyond central California; they are known as the Sierra Madre in Mexico, the Cascades in northern California, Oregon, and Washington, and the mountains of the Aleutian Islands in Alaska. In some of these places, volcanoes are still active.

WHERE VOLCANOES FORM

Because volcanoes form near the meeting of oceanic and continental plates, and the meeting of such plates often forms the edges of continents, volcanoes tend to build near oceans. Most of the world's volcanoes circle the Pacific Ocean in a Ring of Fire—a well-defined, curved line that marks the meeting of many continents and the Pacific Plate.

Volcanoes that are not at plate boundaries—including the Hawaiian volcanoes, which are near the center of a midoceanic plate—are thought to be caused by hot spots, where heat originating deep in the core pushes up through the mantle. The heat burns a narrow vent through the crust under the Pacific Ocean and melts rock that rises and builds into a volcano at the plate's surface. The hot spot remains in one place as the plate moves above it, such as the one creating the string of islands Kauai, Oahu, Molokai, Maui, and Hawaii. Today, the Hawaiian hot spot is believed to be deep beneath the island of Hawaii, fueling Mauna Loa and Kilauea. When hot spots burn up through oceanic plates, only basaltic crust found in ocean floors is available to melt. Resulting volcanic eruptions are sure to be Hawaiian in nature, composed of hot and runny basalt. Hot spots are also found beneath continental plates. The famous hot springs and geysers of Yellowstone National Park in Wyoming probably result from rising magma originating at a hot spot that is similar to the Hawaiian hot spot.

Other midocean volcanoes form where new oceanic plates are created, such as at the Mid-Atlantic Ridge between North America and Europe. New oceanic crust wells up from the mantle and spreads east and west, away from the ridge. Movement of crust is so slow that it is hardly perceptible in a human lifetime. But at these ridges, magma-filled cracks called fissures can open, and basalt floods to the surface. Huge undersea mountains have been building along midocean ridges for millions of years. In some places, the mountains have built high enough to rise above sea level as islands.

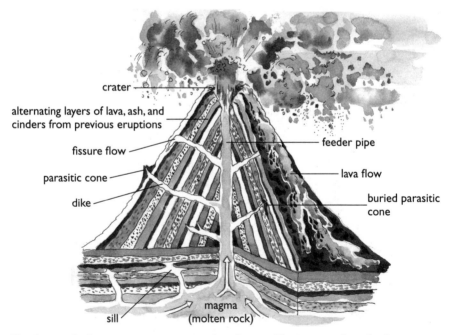

crater

alternating layers of lava, ash, and cinders from previous eruptions

fissure flow

parasitic cone

dike

feeder pipe

lava flow

buried parasitic cone

sill

magma (molten rock)

The shapes of volcanic mountains vary with rock type. Classic, cone-shaped volcanoes are called composite volcanoes, built of alternating layers of ash and lava. Within the volcano are feeder dikes and pipes, through which magma travels.

VOLCANIC SHAPES

As eruption types vary with rock compositions, so shapes of volcanic mountains vary. Thin, hot basaltic lavas in Hawaiian eruptions form gently sloping shield volcanoes, built by thousands of individual lava flows piled on top of each other. Shield volcanoes can build to great heights over many years: Mauna Kea on Hawaii rises 33,476 feet (10,203 meters) above the ocean floor. Alternating layers of ash and lava in varied eruptions build composite volcanoes, the classic volcanic cone shape. Ash or cinder cones result when an eruption is mainly explosive, or pyroclastic; loose material lies in a conical pile around the vent. Craters are funnel-shaped hollows at the mountaintops from which magma erupts; they can enlarge to calderas through collapse or eruption. Very thick magma builds a steep-sided cone as it pushes up like toothpaste from a tube.

TO DO

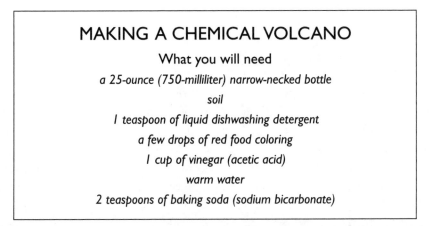

MAKING A CHEMICAL VOLCANO

What you will need

a 25-ounce (750-milliliter) narrow-necked bottle

soil

1 teaspoon of liquid dishwashing detergent

a few drops of red food coloring

1 cup of vinegar (acetic acid)

warm water

2 teaspoons of baking soda (sodium bicarbonate)

This experiment, best done outdoors, shows how the gas in a volcano pushes up and out through its small opening at the top.

Set the bottle on the ground and build a mound of soil up around it. Make the top of your mound about even with the bottle opening to keep the bottle as steady as possible. Shape the dirt to look like any volcano you wish: conical, shield, or composite. If you are unable to go outdoors, work in the sink—volcanic eruptions can be messy.

Pour the detergent into the bottle. Add the drops of food coloring. Add the vinegar, then pour warm water almost to the top. Very quickly add two teaspoons of soda mixed with a little water. Then watch the eruption.

Explanation: The baking soda, which is a base, and the vinegar, which is an acid, react together to release carbon dioxide, a gas. The carbon dioxide gas, which is heavier than air, pushes the mixture from the bottle. Adding detergent helps make more bubbles, simulating frothy, gas-charged lava, and food coloring creates a red-hot appearance.

BAKING VOLCANO TARTS

What you will need

pie crust dough (not puff pastry)

jam

spoon

knife or round cookie cutter

rolling pin

hot pads

muffin tins

A missing component in the chemical volcano experiment described above is heat. Baking volcano tarts shows how heat drives an eruption.

Preheat the oven to 375 degrees. Roll out the pie dough until thin and even. Cut out circles with the knife or cookie cutter to the approximate size of the muffin tin bowls. Put a circle of pie dough in the base of each muffin bowl, and spoon a teaspoon of jam on top. Cover the jam with lids of dough, also cut into circles about the size of the muffin bowls. Press down the edges to seal in the jam. Poke a small hole in the center of each volcano tart with your knife.

Bake the tarts in the preheated oven. Note the changes after 10, 20, and 30 minutes of baking. Continue baking for about 40 minutes or until the jam has erupted out of the tarts. Pull them out of the oven and observe. How has the jam (magma) behaved in the various muffin bowls? Let the volcanic tarts cool before consuming.

Explanation: As it heats up, the jam in the tart builds up pressure until it pours through the hole in the top of the crust. Similarly, a volcano is filled with hot magma that builds up pressure until it pours forth through its vent. In the previous experiment, we saw how the gas content within the magma increases its pressure. In this experiment, we see how heat increases the magma's pressure. In a real volcano, the combination of heat and gas brings on the pressure and eruption.

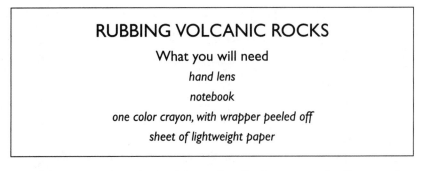

FRACTURING GLASS

What you will need

a few glass marbles

safety glasses

heavy skillet

pot of ice water

metal tongs

hot pad

You can demonstrate how heat makes fractures by cooking marbles on your stove.

Warm the skillet over low heat on your stove. Place the marbles in the skillet, increase the heat, rolling the marbles occasionally with the tongs. Always use the hot pad when handling the tongs or skillet handle, and be sure to wear safety glasses. Watch how the heating affects the marbles.

Next, using the tongs, plunge each marble into the pot of ice water. Do they once again change in appearance, this time from quick cooling? Are the changes deep or on the surface?

Explanation: If solids are not flexible, as glass is not, they can fracture when they expand. The hot rock in volcanoes and geysers usually heats the rocks near them, causing them to crack or break. The resulting fractures fill with magma.

RUBBING VOLCANIC ROCKS

What you will need

hand lens

notebook

one color crayon, with wrapper peeled off

sheet of lightweight paper

Local rocks are used in the building of walls, homes, and offices. Volcanic rocks like basalt make good, dense building materials. Look for volcanic rocks in the walls of your town or city.

If you suspect that volcanic rocks have been used to build a wall, stop and examine it. Look closely with your hand lens. Can you see signs of flow banding, stripes of different colors or textures of rock? Do you see inclusions, different kinds of rocks within the rock? What colors do you see? Describe them in your notebook.

Did the builder of the wall use round or jagged rocks taken straight from the ground? Or are there flat surfaces, showing that the rocks were split? Sketch the shapes of the rocks. Do you see crystals on any of the surfaces? Look closely with your hand lens. Note your observations in your field notebook. Have any surfaces been polished? Polishing is especially common on rocks used in older office buildings. How do those surfaces feel compared with the unpolished ones?

Lay a piece of lightweight paper over an unpolished rock and rub lightly with the side of the peeled crayon. The rubbing will make a good copy of the rock's texture, with all its grains and vesicles, or air holes. You may want to tape the rubbing in your field notebook. Collect rubbings made of various rocks in different colors—they are excellent for use in collages.

Explanation: To make a neat pile, wall builders often split rocks along planes of weakness. In volcanic rocks, such weak planes may follow the direction of flow banding. Such banding forms while magma flows, stretching and pulling minerals that are still molten in the thick lava. Sometimes quartz or other mineral crystals line the planes of weakness and can be seen where the rocks are split.

The different colors are due to the different minerals in the rocks. Colors of minerals change with weathering but are still important to observe and record.

VISITING A VOLCANO

What you will need

hand lens

notebook

There are many things to observe near inactive volcanoes, sometimes found in national parks and forests.

Before your trip, find out what mountain range you will be visiting (ask at home, school, or the library), and research whether volcanoes in the range are active. At the volcanic landscape, look for signs of life. If you do not see any right away, check the rocks carefully for signs of lichen or very small plants. Consider how life began on the rocks and what will happen next.

Check for rocks near the path. Look to see if they are dark or light colored and if the minerals within them are small or large. Rocks that have erupted suddenly from the earth tend to be very fine grained.

Study the shapes of any peaks you see while you hike. Are they round, spirelike, or cone shaped?

Explanation: Volcanic eruptions tend to destroy life surrounding their mountains by covering the landscape with hot rock and filling the air with gases other than oxygen. Biological species will return to the volcano eventually; but it can take hundreds to thousands of years. Clues to finding volcanic mountains can include their cone shapes and exposures of fine-grained rock.

Here are some other facts to know when studying volcanic landscapes.

Volcanic mountains:
- Sometimes stand alone
- Are sometimes shaped like cones
- Are often found within a few hundred miles of a coastline
- Are often found on islands

Volcanic rocks:
- Are sometimes riddled with vesicles, or air bubbles
- Are made of fine-grained minerals
- May be glassy (if obsidian)
- May float (if pumice)

Look for the following characteristics when trying to distinguish among common types of volcanic rocks.

Basalt:
- Is common in Hawaiian eruptions
- Is often filled with holes made by trapped gases
- Is fine grained
- Has ropy or blocky texture from slow or broken flow
- Is black or dark green in color, containing large amounts of the iron- and magnesium-rich mineral pyroxene
- Contains only small amounts of the mineral quartz, because the magma has little silica

Andesite:
- Is common in volcanoes found at the boundaries between oceanic and continental plates
- Is fine grained
- Has overall blocky texture resulting from a thick lava flow
- Is generally gray, green, or red in color, weathering to dark or reddish brown
- Contains some quartz

Rhyolite:

- Is light colored, quartz rich
- Often shows flow lines or banding, where minerals have been stretched while hot, in the direction the lava has traveled
- Crystallizes from slow-moving, viscous lavas
- Has the same chemical composition as granite, which is very rich in silica and contains much quartz

---

SEEING HOW PUMICE FLOATS

What you will need

dry sponge

tub of water

Pumice, a type of volcanic rock, is light enough to float. Air within the rock keeps pumice afloat. To see how the air in pumice works to keep the rock afloat, try the following simple experiment.

Take the dry sponge to the water when you bathe or swim. Notice that the sponge floats, especially when dry, but even when wet. Where does the water go in a soaked sponge? If a sponge is getting wet and soggy, why does it still float?

Explanation: Pumice is made up more of air spaces than of rock. Pumice floats like a sponge because, even though water enters some of the vesicles, or air holes, it cannot enter all the vesicles to sink the rock. Other volcanic rocks do not float, because they have fewer vesicles and so are made up more of rock than of air.

You can also try this experiment with pumice sold at rock shops and hardware stores.

MAPPING VOLCANOES

What you will need

detailed map of the world

package of stick-on dots

Many of the world's volcanoes form a great circle around the Pacific Ocean known as the Ring of Fire. Finding the volcanoes on a map of the world illustrates just how closely the ring follows the edge of continents.

Look for the mountains listed below on a globe or map of the world. Mark each mountain with a stick-on dot. If you are not able to mark the map, find the mountains and sketch their positions in your field notebook. Do you know the names of some others? If so, make note of them too.

Tarawera, New Zealand	Katmai, Alaska
Ulawun, Madura	Rainier, Washington
Taal, Philippines	St. Helens, Washington
Mayon, Philippines	Shasta, California
Krakatoa, Indonesia	Adams, Washington
Sinabung, Indonesia	Lassen, California
Fuji, Japan	Paricutín, Mexico
Bezymianny, Kamchatka	Irazu, Costa Rica
Shishaldin, Alaska	Cotopaxi, Ecuador
Mauna Loa, Hawaii	El Misti, Peru
Kilauea, Hawaii	Azul, Argentina
Surtsey, Iceland	Pelée, Martinique
Hekla, Iceland	Fogo, Cape Verde Islands
La Palma, Canary Islands	

Explanation: These mountains are some of the five hundred active volcanoes in the world. Many lie along the Ring of Fire. Others are at hot spots. To be considered active, a volcano must have erupted at least once within recorded history. Fifty active volcanoes are in the United States—in Alaska, California, Hawaii, Oregon, and Washington.

SODA POP!

What you will need

can of soda

lots of outdoor space

Experimenting with canned soda is easy and gives a good illustration of volcanic activity.

Carbon dioxide gas is trapped within a can of soda, just as gases are trapped within a volcano that is building toward an eruption.

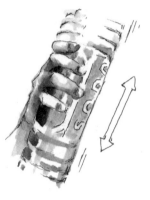

Shaking the soda increases the effect of gas content in the can, just as gases expand in hot magma rising in the earth.

When you pop the top, you release the gases, just as a volcanic eruption blasts gas far and wide in Vesuvian-style volcanoes.

The gas-filled bubbles streaming down the can are much like a nuée ardente that charges down a mountainside on a cloud of gas.

Give the can a good shake, then, holding the soda as far from you as possible, quickly pull the top open and watch what erupts.

Explanation: The thickness of a magma determines how explosive a volcanic eruption will be, but so does the magma's gas content. Two identical magmas will erupt differently if one has more trapped gases than the other. Inside the can of soda, carbon dioxide gas is trapped and cannot expand, as gases are trapped within a volcano that has not yet erupted.

As you shake the soda, most of the gaseous carbon dioxide in the can disolves in the liquid, like trapped gases in magma. When you pop the top, the soda shoots out of the can, driven by the expansion of gases. A very vigorous shake will bring on a Vesuvian eruption of soda pop—gas will work out of the soda and blast far and high when released, much like the air-fall ash and pumice from Vesuvius and Mount St. Helens. The remaining foamy soda will climb out of and run down the can as gas-filled bubbles, much like the *nuée ardente* that charged down Mount Pelée.

Do you think warm soda will erupt more violently than cold soda? Will different sodas erupt differently?

TO THINK ABOUT

Dionisio's Field. On February 20, 1943, Mexican farmer Dionisio Pulido was plowing his field when the earth suddenly rumbled beneath him. The ground swelled and burst open, and whistling steam, fire, and the strong smell of sulfur rose from the ground. Dionisio ran to the nearby town, Paricutín, for help. The next morning, when he returned to his field, it was no longer there. In its place sat a 30-foot (9-meter) high cone of ash and stone. By noon the cone had risen to 150 feet (45 meters). After a week, it was 450 feet (135 meters) high.

What was happening in Dionisio's field? The people soon realized that a volcano was rapidly building. Would you have evacuated the town a mile away, as the people of Paricutín did? What would you expect to happen next? Could you have guessed that the entire town would be buried in lava and the volcano would reach 1,500 feet (450 meters) in a year?

Harry Truman of Mount St. Helens. When Mount St. Helens in Washington State erupted on May 18, 1980, dozens of people were killed. Many had been warned of the mountain's danger; one was a geologist at a nearby outpost. One elderly man who was killed, Harry Truman, lived at Mount St. Helens Lodge on Spirit Lake, beneath the mountain's summit. Mr. Truman, although warned of the probable eruption, felt he could not leave his longtime home. "I am part of that mountain," he said. "The mountain is part of me."

If you knew your home would soon be destroyed, how would you feel? Would you leave or stay?

Tools of Glass. Earlier civilizations used obsidian, fine-grained volcanic glass, to make sharp tools and weapons. Obsidian is dark in color because it contains microscopic particles of dark minerals, and it is usually similar in

For generations of visitors, Spirit Lake, at the foot of majestic Mount St. Helens, was a popular, peaceful vacation spot.

On May 18, 1980, an eruption blasted away the north side of the peak, setting off massive landslides.

Forests over a 232-square-mile (600-square-kilometer) area were flattened by the blast, burying Spirit Lake and all its surrounding homes and lodges under 200 feet (60 meters) of mud and debris.

DISCOVER NATURE IN THE ROCKS

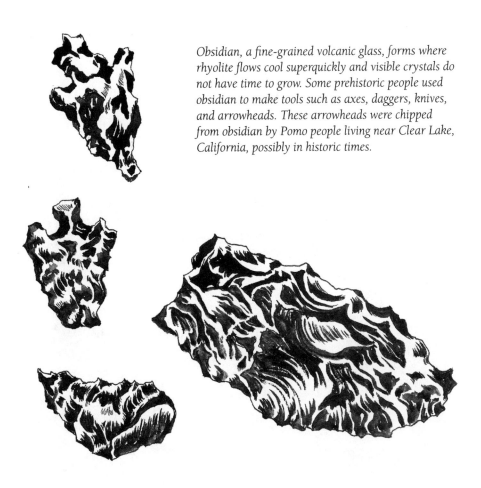

Obsidian, a fine-grained volcanic glass, forms where rhyolite flows cool superquickly and visible crystals do not have time to grow. Some prehistoric people used obsidian to make tools such as axes, daggers, knives, and arrowheads. These arrowheads were chipped from obsidian by Pomo people living near Clear Lake, California, possibly in historic times.

composition to rhyolite and granite. Obsidian forms on the outer skin of rhyolite flows, where lava cools superquickly, too quickly for crystals to form.

Obsidian has conchoidal fracture and is sharp and jagged on its edges. Early toolmakers took advantage of these fractures, breaking chips from larger chunks of rock that they transformed into sharp-edged axes, daggers, knives, and arrowheads. Often these tools were attached to wooden spears, arrow shafts, and axe handles.

TO READ

"Crucibles of Creation: Volcanoes," *National Geographic* 182, no. 6; 5–41 (1992). This article shows spectacular color and black-and-white photographs of volcanoes with details of famous eruptions.

Du Bois, William Pene. *The Twenty-One Balloons.* New York: The Viking Press,

1947. Outstanding juvenile fiction about life on Krakatoa until the eruption in 1883.

Francis, Peter. *Volcanoes*. Middlesex, England: Penguin Books, 1976. This highly readable book describes classic eruptions, volcanic processes, and volcanic rocks.

Tilling, Robert I. *Volcanoes*. Washington, DC: U.S. Government Printing Office, 1982. The U.S. Geological Survey's pamphlet on volcanoes is a classic publication with historic black-and-white photographs.

TO WATCH

Eruption at Sea. Ka'io Productions, 1990. Close-up footage of Hawaiian volcanic processes and explanations of lava tubes and shield volcanoes.

Inside Hawaiian Volcanoes. Smithsonian Institution–United States Geological Survey, 1989. Animation, graphics, and film footage tell a well-rounded story of volcanoes in Hawaii.

Volcanoes: Too Hot to Handle. Children's Television Workshop, 1991. The "3-2-1 Contact" kids visit a Hawaiian volcano and Mount St. Helens.

CHAPTER 4

Sediment: Piecing Rock Together

S edimentary rocks make up as much as 70 percent of all rocks on the earth's surface. The large percentage with respect to the other two rock types, igneous and metamorphic, may seem disproportionate until you consider that igneous and metamorphic processes take place far below the ground. In contrast, deposition, the laying down of sedimentary particles, is always at work on the earth's surface, as are the processes of erosion—the physical and chemical breaking down of rocks into particles. Solid rock is constantly being torn down, only to have its pieces carried elsewhere. Wind carves out cliffs of rock and transports its fragments off as dust. Rainwater picks up sand and silt, moving them to ditches and creeks. Rivers carry rocks and sand downstream through their valleys to settle into lakes or wash out to sea. Lake mud, river gravel, beach sand, porch dust—all are sediments brought from elsewhere to settle and accumulate.

The transporting mode for the sedimentary particles—wind, water, or gravity—has more energy at the source area than at the area of deposition. The wind may pick up sand particles, but when it loses energy and dies down, it drops the sand. Boulders may be pulled down steep hillsides by the force of gravity, but on the level surfaces farther down the slopes, the boulders lose momentum and stop. Cobbles may be carried down a mountain by the movement of a glacier or by flowing creek water, but when the glacier halts or the creek flow wanes, the cobbles drop out. In these ways, because of decreased energy in the modes of transportation, the particles settle in their places of deposition, either to be buried layer upon layer and become sedimentary rock or to be picked up again, perhaps by a river in flood or by an advancing glacier.

LAWS OF SEDIMENTATION

Two important geologic laws of deposition help us understand sedimentary rocks. The laws were proposed in 1669 by Danish physician Niels Stenson, also known as Nicholas Steno, who studied fossils in Italy. Although they were not generally accepted by geologists for a few hundred years, Steno's laws are recognized today as important foundations of the science of geology.

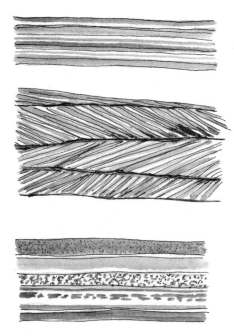

Steno's law of original horizontality states that sediments are deposited in horizontal layers parallel or nearly parallel to the ground.

Cross-bedding in sandstones forms at angles to bedding planes that are generally horizontal and parallel to the ground.

Steno's law of superposition states that younger sediments are deposited on top of older sediments. The bottom layer in this drawing, perhaps a massive unit of limestone, is probably the oldest. The stippled top layer, a sandstone, is probably younger than underlying layers, which grade from older to younger from bottom to top.

DISCOVER NATURE IN THE ROCKS

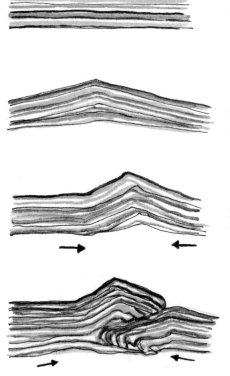

Sedimentary layers are deposited according to the law of original horizontality.

Layers are beginning to buckle as crustal plate movement applies pressure at either end of the layers.

Steeper contours in the layers occur as pressure increases.

Continued pressure results in layers being uplifted, buckled, and broken so that some older beds are placed above younger.

The first is the law of original horizontality, which says that sediments are deposited in horizontal layers, or beds, parallel or nearly parallel to ground surface. If we see sedimentary rocks at an angle to the horizontal surface of the earth, we can assume they have been disturbed or tilted by strong forces of compression since their deposition. Certain sedimentary rocks, especially sandstones, may show internal layering at an angle to the overall bed of rock. The angled bedding is called cross-bedding, which results from the movement of particles down dune faces, especially in deserts and on beaches. Although cross-bedding may not be parallel to the earth's surface, the layers of rock in which it is found usually are.

The second of Steno's laws is the principle of superposition, which says that younger sedimentary beds are deposited on top of older beds. According to this principle, layers of sediments are arranged from older to younger, from bottom to top, in any sequence of deposited beds. Learning about superposition is essential to understanding which rocks are younger in any environment. As in the law of original horizontality, exceptions can be found: Older sediments may lie above younger sediments when beds have been intensely folded by mountain building or other great forces. Or younger sediments may be deposited beneath older sediments in unusual circumstances (see "To Think About" later in this chapter). If we apply Steno's laws with great care and intelligence, however, they serve well in our study of sedimentary rocks.

Many prime examples of both laws are found in the rocks of the Grand Canyon, one of the earth's most spectacular geologic displays. Geologists have studied the sedimentary beds and fossils in the canyon to such an extent that the ages and layers are well understood. Younger sedimentary rocks overlie older sedimentary rocks, clearly visible because the layers have been cut through and exposed by erosion. In several places in the canyon, horizontal beds of sediments overlie tilted beds of sediments that were moved and

In the Grand Canyon, younger sedimentary rocks clearly overlie older rocks. This view of the canyon shows the Inner Gorge of Precambrian schist (1.2 to 1.7 billion years old) directly overlain by Cambrian Tapeats Sandstone (about 550 million years old). Above the Tapeats Sandstone are layers of progressively younger sedimentary rocks, from 500 million to 250 million years old.

DISCOVER NATURE IN THE ROCKS

Much time elapsed after the deposition of the sedimentary rocks that later metamorphosed to schist in the Inner Gorge of the Grand Canyon. The rocks, originally sediments deposited horizontally, were altered and uplifted. Later, when the entire area subsided and seawater covered the altered rocks, more sediments were deposited. Sediments deposited much later therefore rest horizontally above the older tilted rocks.

uplifted from their originally horizontal positions by pressure created by crustal movement before the younger rocks were deposited. As scientists continue to study sedimentary layers in the canyon and elsewhere, Steno's laws not only hold true but consistently prove useful.

NAMING SEDIMENTARY ROCKS

Sedimentary rocks are named for the particles that compose them. The particles fall into three general categories: clastic, chemical, and biogenic. Because these materials vary widely, sedimentary rocks vary, too, in terms of appearance and composition.

Clastic Sediments. Clastic sedimentary rocks are those made of fragments of older rocks. The fragments are called clasts, a name derived from the Greek word *klastos*, which means broken. Clasts may be as large as house-sized boulders or as small as submicroscopic clay pieces. Clast size helps define and name clastic sedimentary rocks. If a rock contains mostly large clasts, such as boulders, cobbles, and pebbles, it is a conglomerate or breccia. If it contains mostly sand, it is a sandstone. If it contains mostly clay particles,

clast chart

Particle		Diameter Size in millimeters (mm)	Rock Name
Gravel	Boulder	More than 256 mm	Conglomerate and breccia
	Cobble	64 to 256 mm	
	Pebble	2 to 64 mm	
Sand		$1/16$ to 2 mm	Sandstone
Silt		$1/256$ to $1/16$ mm	Siltstone
Clay		Less than $1/256$ mm	Mudstone and shale

Use this clast chart to identify sedimentary rocks and the particles that compose them.

it is a mudstone or shale. A quick look at a clast chart, such as the one in this chapter, distinguishes sedimentary rocks on the basis of the majority of certain-sized clasts they contain.

Once a rock is defined in terms of clast size, the clasts themselves must be described. Are they rounded or angular? Are they of one size or many—that is, are the clasts well sorted into a single size group or not? Are the clasts arranged in layers or jumbled into chaotic disarray? What are the clasts made of—sandstone, limestone, volcanic rock? Evaluating clastic sedimentary rocks is a matter of describing all that can be observed about the clasts, each observation giving a clue to how the rock was made.

Chemical Sediments. Chemical sedimentary rocks contain no clasts. The material in chemical sediments has been transported from elsewhere, but not as distinct particles moved by erosive forces. Rather, the material has moved as dissolved chemicals in solution. When the solution becomes too full of the chemicals, they precipitate as chemical sedimentary material. One example of

sorting and roundness

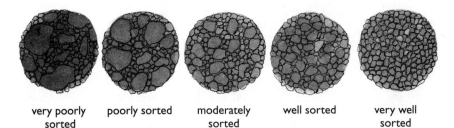

| very poorly sorted | poorly sorted | moderately sorted | well sorted | very well sorted |

Well-sorted sediments contain clasts of nearly equal sizes. Poorly sorted sediments contain clasts of many sizes.

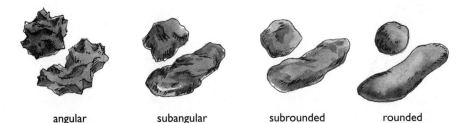

| angular | subangular | subrounded | rounded |

Clasts range from angular to rounded depending on how many sharp edges have been worn off by erosion and abrasion.

Yellowstone National Park has fantastic pools and spires formed by hot-water mineral deposition.

chemical sedimentation takes place in ocean or lake water that is high in salts. As some water evaporates, the salts become more concentrated in the water that remains. The concentrated salts subsequently crystallize into such minerals as halite (table salt) and gypsum.

Sediments also form when chemical reactions occur within solutions. In seawater, certain microscopic plants cause chemical changes around them, bringing about the deposition of the mineral calcite. In some homes, chemical-rich water deposits the mineral calcite in hot-water pipes. At the edges of hot springs, cooler water often deposits the minerals calcite and opal, which form crusts that may be white or multicolored. There are good examples of hot-water mineral deposition in Yellowstone National Park.

Biogenic Sediments. Biogenic sedimentary rocks consist mostly of the remains of plants and animals that have died, accumulated, and been preserved. Biogenic rocks fall into two categories: bioclastic and organic.

Bioclastic biogenic rocks contain clasts of organisms, the broken pieces of shells and skeletons of once-living creatures. The clasts are deposited over time, usually in lakes and oceans. The biogenic sediment that accumulates on the lake or ocean floor may contain calcite-rich clasts, such as bits of coral, or silica-rich clasts, such as pieces of sponges. In either case, because the clasts are pieces of once-living beings, they are bioclasts. The resulting sedimentary rocks are considered bioclastic.

Organic biogenic rocks contain organic substances, comprising the elements carbon and hydrogen. When these organic substances are trapped in sediments so that they cannot completely decay, they break down only partially, becoming fossil fuels such as coal, oil, and natural gas. Rocks that contain significant amounts of any of these fossil fuels are called organic sedimentary rocks.

DEPOSITIONAL ENVIRONMENTS

Although the final destination of all sedimentary material is the ocean floor, where the bulk of the earth's sedimentary rocks are found, the material may be deposited first in other environments where the transporting agents wind, water, and ice are at work.

Rivers. Rivers are the chief means of transportation for sediments across the land. Igneous, metamorphic, or sedimentary rock material is picked up from a source area, such as a mountain range, by lively young streams with steeply sloped courses. From there, the material is carried farther downstream. Where sedimentary material is deposited depends on the river's energy—how much water travels through the river and how swiftly it moves. A high-energy stream, with plenty of water moving quickly, can carry larger clasts than a low-energy stream. As a stream's energy wanes, say while dropping from flood stage to normal flow, it deposits its larger clasts. As a stream's energy wanes further, it deposits even the smaller clasts.

A river often deposits its large and small clasts in different reaches, or stretches, along its length. In its upstream reaches, a river may braid in a series of lively channels, dropping boulders and cobbles that pile up into islands between the channels. Farther downstream, where the river may wind in wandering loops called meanders, sand clasts deposit in inner bends where the current runs more slowly. In slow reaches where water ponding and smoother flow can occur, even the finest particles such as silt and clay drop out of the moving water.

River deposits, therefore, can be coarse-grained gravels or fine-grained sand, silt, and clay. Often, river-deposited sedimentary rocks will consist of both fine-grained (small-sized) clasts and coarse-grained (large-sized) clasts. The various-sized clasts tend to accumulate in layers—layers of fine material will alternate with layers of coarse material. Examine any riverbank to see the well-sorted, alternating layers of cobbles, sand, and silt deposited by the river

river and delta

A river may originate at the toe of a melting glacier, beginning as a series of high-energy braided streams dropping from steep mountain courses. Braided streams move rapidly and can carry large clasts. As the river flows downstream, moving into gentler terrain, it slows down, dropping successively smaller clasts. The slowing river moves in wide loops, or meanders.

Where the river meets the ocean, finer clasts—sand, silt, and clay—are deposited in a fan-shaped delta and along the ocean shore, forming beaches.

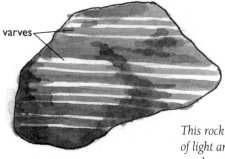

varves

This rock sample displays varves, the fine striations of light and dark deposits in lake beds. Dark bands are deposited in winter, light bands in summer.

as it meandered and changed course. Sandstones, shales, and conglomerates are a few of the rocks that can be found in ancient riverbeds.

Lakes. Sediments reach lakes by the action of rivers, by wind moving over the land, and out of the melting ice of glaciers. Sediments deposited in lakes settle either along shore or on the lake floor. Shore deposits can be beach sands and silts, if carried by moderate to gentle currents along the shore, or gravels, if carried onto shore by higher-energy wave action. Lake floor sediments are extremely fine grained, moved into the depths by slow-moving currents incapable of carrying anything but the smallest, lightest sediments. They settle in thin, even, well-sorted layers. In regions with well-defined seasons, the layers may alternate in bands of dark and light colors, depending on the conditions in which they were deposited. In winter, when lakes are iced over, only the finest sediments still contained in the waters after freeze-up will settle out, and dark, fine-grained bands of clay and silt result. In summer, when streams bring in surges of coarser-grained material such as sand, lighter-colored bands of sediment develop on lake bottoms. Rocks formed from lake deposits display fine black and white stripes, or varves. Shales are also found in ancient lake beds.

Glaciers. Sedimentary material can be gouged from a landscape and carried downhill by glaciers. The material accumulates at the edges of the ice or even farther down the slope, carried by running water from glacier melt. The rocks in glacial deposits usually contain poorly sorted clasts and few layers. Till, the random mixture of rock fragments plastered directly onto the ground from the base of the ice, is a common glacial sedimentary deposit. Particles in till can range from clay to boulder sized. Glacial debris is also deposited as moraines, accumulations of sediment pushed by the ice. Moraines may be found in piles left beneath, beside, and at the ends of glaciers.

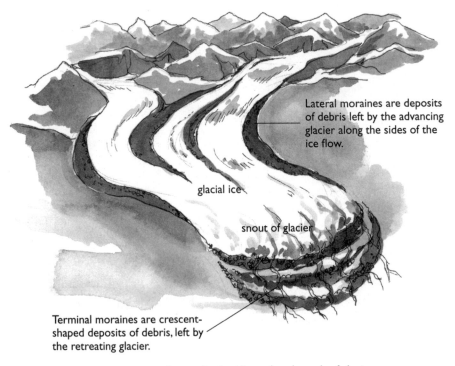

Lateral moraines are deposits of debris left by the advancing glacier along the sides of the ice flow.

glacial ice

snout of glacier

Terminal moraines are crescent-shaped deposits of debris, left by the retreating glacier.

Moraines accumulate under, beside, and at the ends of glaciers.

Wind. Particles of sediment may be moved by strong winds, especially in deserts and along seacoasts. In those environments, plants are sparse, unable to either act as windbreaks or hold clasts of soil and sediment stable on the ground surface. As a result, particles can be picked up by the wind and carried to better protected areas, where they may be deposited. The resulting deposits, named aeolian for Aeolus, Greek god of wind, are usually thick beds of sandstone, fine grained and well sorted, composed only of small and light particles.

Aeolian deposits tend to accumulate in the shapes of dunes, hills of sand with gently sloping upwind faces and steeply sloping downwind faces. The individual grains of sand within the dunes show fine pitting, or frosting, on their surfaces, like the sandblasted coatings seen on pieces of glass found on beaches. Scientists have attributed the frosted look to everything from the dissolving action of dew to cracking and scoring from repeated impact against other grains. Geologists can identify wind deposits from these two attributes, dune shapes and frosted sand grains, as well as cross-bedding within layers.

Oceans. As rivers carry sediment downstream to the sea, it is deposited near shore beyond the river mouths, moved along the coast by currents, or carried farther out to sea, eventually to settle on the ocean floor. Each type of sediment movement creates unique landforms and deposits in the rock record, because each environment has different forces at work. Sediments deposited at the mouths of rivers build out into deltas, named for the Greek letter delta (Δ) because of their roughly triangular shapes created by many branching channels. Deltas often form where rivers meet oceans as streams flowing into standing water slow down and drop their loads of sediment. Delta deposits in the rock record are a mix of silty sand where the river channel extended past shore, finer-grained clayey silt that built islands between channels, and even finer-grained silty clay that was carried farther out to sea, to the farthest reaches of the delta.

Sediments can be moved along shore by ocean currents because strong currents, known as longshore currents, work parallel to the seacoast. The resulting beach deposits may contain sand and coarser clasts washed from either rivers or nearby rocky cliffs. The sand travels parallel to the shore to settle in elongate beaches and sandy spits that extend from the beaches. The coarser material settles closer to its source, be it river mouth or rocky cliff. Waves working over the beach surface drag both sand and rock particles back and forth, rounding them by abrasion.

The finest-grained sediment carried by rivers moves beyond the river mouth, beyond the delta, away from the beaches, to settle on the ocean floor. It settles mainly on the continental shelves, submerged extensions of the continents that form undersea platforms offshore. Most ocean deposits are found on the shelves. Over the past 70 to 100 million years, about 9 miles (14 kilometers) of sediment has accumulated on the shelves, making up mudstones that form the great bulk of the earth's sedimentary rocks.

Beyond the shelves lies the deep sea. Only 10 percent of sediment that reaches the continental shelves is carried past them to the deep sea. Rates at

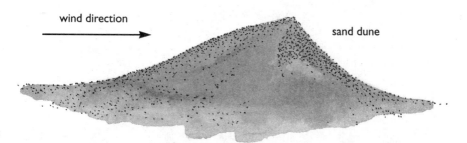

Dunes are hills of sand with gently sloping upwind faces and steeply sloping downwind faces. In this drawing of a wind-deposited sand dune, direction of wind travel was from left to right.

which sediment can be deposited on the deep-sea floor are very slow, because little sediment reaches this part of the sea. Much of the sediment that does reach the deep sea is easily dissolved in the high-pressure, cold ocean waters.

TURNING TO STONE

Sediments become rock through the work of chemical, physical, and biological processes. Not as drastic as metamorphism, the processes taken together are known as diagenesis, another word with Greek roots (from *dia,* which means "through," and *gignesthai,* "to be born"). Diagenesis brings rock forth from sediment through the action of compaction, cementation, and chemical changes.

Compaction occurs as sediments pile up and force underlying grains together through the sheer weight of burial. Cementation occurs as mineral-laden water circulates among sedimentary particles and cements them together. Chemical changes can occur within sediments as less stable minerals convert to more stable forms, as when the mineral aragonite, which makes up the skeletons of living corals, over time transforms to the related mineral calcite. Chemical changes can also occur in sediments both in and out of the presence of oxygen. When oxygen is available within accumulating sediments, organic remains decay to carbon dioxide and water. When oxygen is not available, decay is incomplete, instead transforming organic remains to carbon, and forming coal, oil, and natural gas.

Through these and other processes, sediments become rocks. The resulting sedimentary rocks are in turn available for erosion and transportation once again as clasts in the great rock cycle.

TO DO

MODELING SEDIMENTARY LAYERS

What you will need

clear glass jar with a lid

¼ cup large dried lima beans

¼ cup dried pinto beans

¼ cup uncooked rice

¼ cup crushed Rice Krispies, bran flakes, or other cereal

tap water

clock, watch, or timer

notebook

You can make a model of sedimentary layers using materials from your kitchen and the grocery store.

Place all the ingredients, one at a time, into a glass jar. (The jar must be big enough to hold all the ingredients, water, and 2 inches [5 centimeters] of air below the lid.) Add water to the jar until the ingredients are covered. Screw the lid on securely and shake the jar.

Set the jar on a flat surface and do not disturb. Observe what happens to the ingredients in the jar. Record your observations beginning 1 minute after shaking. Continue observing for 15 minutes, recording observations at 3-minute intervals. Note how long it takes the various particles to settle, which settle first, how they look as they settle, and how grain sizes change from layer to layer. Compare the number of layers to the number of ingredients used in preparing the experiment.

Explanation: Heavy (large or dense) particles settle through water more readily than light (small or not dense) particles. If heavy and light particles are mixed in still water, the heavier particles will settle first, creating a bottom layer above which the lighter particles settle. Because the particles take different amounts of time to settle, they are said to have different settling rates. The transition of heavy to light particles from bottom to top is called grading.

Whenever you observe sedimentary layers of different-sized particles in the outdoors, relate your observations to the layers in the jar. You can visualize the sedimentary particles settling out of lake or river water in much the same way. A modern illustration such as the dried ingredients settling in the jar helps in understanding past geologic events.

DIGGING UP DIRT

What you will need

shovel

hand lens

measuring tape

notebook

You can learn about layers of earth by digging a hole in the ground near your home.

In your garden or yard, dig a hole large enough to display the layers of earth beneath your feet. Make sure the hole is in a safe place so that no people or pets will fall in while you work. While digging, notice changes in the ground's hardness as you go deeper. Measure the depth and width of your excavation with the measuring tape.

Sketch any changes in the earth's color and texture in your notebook. Note layers in the earthen sides of the hole, their thickness, whether the earth is wet or dry, whether there are pieces of broken rock, and when, if ever, you reach a thick layer of rock you cannot penetrate. Using your hand lens, study samples of the different materials more closely.

Explanation: Although we often think of the stuff in our gardens simply as dirt, it is more accurately called soil and rock. Soil is the relatively loose upper layer of earth that may be dug or plowed and in which plants grow. It is the weathered product of underlying rock. As soil, the rock has decomposed enough for plants to take root in, draw water through, and absorb nutrients from the breakdown of minerals in the rock.

The upper dark layer of 6 to 8 inches (15 to 20 centimeters) is topsoil, rich in humus, a dark material resulting from the decomposition of plants and animals. In some parts of the world, topsoil can be 6 feet (almost 2 meters) deep. Below the topsoil lies the more compact and less fertile subsoil. It is lighter in color, not as rich in decomposed organic matter. Beneath the subsoil lies the parent material, the rock from which soil is derived—either broken rock or bedrock, the final and lowest layer any casual hole digger can reach.

COLLECTING SAND

What you will need

zipper-sealing plastic bags

masking tape to label bags

hand lens

magnet

clast charts

notebook

If you look closely at the sand at the coast, river, lake, or playground, you can analyze the type of rock the sand came from.

Collect sand in small amounts from various beaches and sandboxes. Keep your sand samples separate by sealing them in plastic bags. Label each bag with the date and location of sample collection. Using your hand lens, look closely at each sample. Describe it in terms of color, roundness, and clast size. Guess what types of rock the particles came from.

Explanation: The color of beach sand depends on the color of its parent rock. In the United States, much of the beach sand is gray, composed of tiny particles of disintegrated granite. Some Florida beaches are expanses of white sand, made of minute bits of broken coral. Hawaii has black and green sand beaches of volcanic rock particles. Some black sand beaches are composed of tiny iron particles rather than bits of volcanic rock; you can test this with a magnet. The iron particles will be picked up easily with the magnet; other minerals will not. Other clast colors you may observe in sand include light brown (pieces of granite or quartz), yellow (quartz), gold (mica), red (garnet), and pink (feldspar).

Sand collected from playgrounds is usually light gray in color, derived from granitic rock. It has probably been cleaned and screened through a sieve and so is well sorted by size.

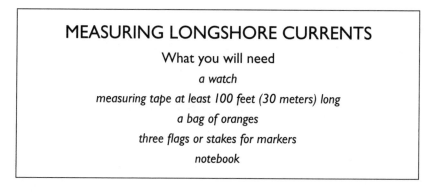

MEASURING LONGSHORE CURRENTS

What you will need

a watch

measuring tape at least 100 feet (30 meters) long

a bag of oranges

three flags or stakes for markers

notebook

This experiment with sea currents that parallel the shoreline requires a trip to the coast.

Choose a point on shore to begin the experiment. The beginning point should be near the water but out of reach of wave action. Set the first marker flag or stake at your chosen beginning point. Measure 100 feet (30 meters) in both directions parallel to the shoreline. Set the other markers at the endpoints.

From the beginning point, throw two oranges straight out into the ocean. (This part of the experiment requires either the help of a friend or closely spaced tosses by you, because the oranges should be timed to hit the water nearly simultaneously.) One orange should land in the surf zone of the breaking waves. The second should land on the seaward side of the breaking waves, past the surf zone and as far out as possible.

Using your watch, begin timing the floating oranges as soon as they hit the water. Stop timing them when they pass either endpoint. Note how long they took to travel to the endpoints. Note also which direction the oranges floated and which orange floated fastest. You can calculate the velocity (speed) of the currents that carried the oranges by dividing the distance traveled by the time it took: velocity = distance ÷ time. Thus if an orange travels 100 feet (30 meters) in 50 seconds, current speed equals 2 feet (about .5 meters) per second. Repeat the experiment as many times as you wish to gather data. Try conducting the experiment five times and recalculating the velocity each time. Note the direction and velocity of the currents, the direction in which they travel, and which current is fastest—that in the surf zone or that farther out to sea.

Explanation: In the ocean, longshore currents travel parallel to shore. The currents are generated by waves breaking at an angle to the coast. Longshore currents are strongest in the surf zone and weaker farther out to sea. Sediment is carried by the longshore currents, developing sedimentary coastal features that reflect the direction of water flow.

Natural sand spits, sand accumulating on the upcurrent sides of engineered jetties and harbor arms, and sediment carried downshore from stream mouths are all phenomena resulting from longshore currents.

TO THINK ABOUT

Sedimentary Reefs. A reef is a chain of rocks or sand that lies near the surface of a body of water. Because it is barely submerged, a reef may pose a hazard to boat navigation. In the ocean, a reef acts as a protective wave buffer, breaking the destructive action of surf before it reaches shore. Today's prominent reefs—the Great Barrier Reef in Australia, the Belize Barrier and Atoll Reefs, coral reefs in Jamaica and elsewhere—provide living examples of how reefs developed in the past.

Modern reefs build up at the edges of offshore platforms, in warm, shallow waters. Most reefs are constructed of upwardly growing corals, which are calcareous skeletal structures that protect small, soft organisms living within. Fish, sponges, clams, barnacles, worms, snails, and other ocean organisms break down the coral's skeletal structure by boring into it, grazing for food on its surface, or grinding away pieces of coral. Broken bits of the structure settle in the surrounding spaces. Although the standing coral skeletons may remain in place after the death of the organisms within, storms may eventually topple them. Fine-grained sediment will cover them. Through the living, dying, and accumulating of coral pieces and other sediment, the reef grows.

Geologists have found huge fossil reef deposits in limestones in the world's rock record. Because they are composed of various types of sediment and expired organisms, fossil reefs vary widely in appearance. The fossil coral colonies appear porous. Fine-grained sediments often fill in the cavities.

Fossil reefs buried by overlying sediment contain unusually large amounts of oil and natural gas as compared with other sedimentary deposits. For this reason, reef deposits have been studied in great detail by geologists in search of underground oil. Some of North America's great petroleum-producing reef deposits lie in the United States in Colorado, Texas, and Utah and in Canada in Alberta. Other great fossil reefs are in southeastern Spain and on the lower slopes of the Italian Alps.

Understanding Facies. We often describe sedimentary rocks solely in a strong vertical sense, observing changes from layer to layer. But sedimentary rocks also display changes in their horizontal planes. Within a single layer, sediments may change from conglomerate to sandstone to shale to limestone. Each rock type was deposited in a specific environment, but over horizontal distance the environments changed. The layer of rock may consist of varied ocean sediments where sandstones were deposited near shore, shales deposited farther out, and calcareous oozes formed on the platforms. Each distinctive deposit within the horizontal layer is called a facies, a unique type of sedimentary rock within deposits of the same age. Changes in facies are caused by variations in the environment of deposition at a given time.

The Grand Canyon is an excellent place to study facies changes within layers, because continuous layers are well exposed over great distances. A geologic map of the canyon shows many long, jagged lines of color that can be traced from one end of the map to the other. Each line of color represents a bed of rock, which has the same name everywhere on the map. In the real rocks, however, although the names of layers may be the same, changes and different characteristics appear as we traverse the horizontal miles along the rock layers. A rock unit called the Bright Angel Shale, visible in most parts of the canyon, contains more limestone and dolomite in the western end of the canyon, near Lake Mead, than in the eastern end near the Little Colorado. An overlying unit, the Muav Limestone, contains almost all limestone and dolomite in the west and sandstones and shales in the east. These deposits, laid down by the waters of an ancient inland ocean, show facies changes representative of different environments within the ocean: limestones and dolomites in shallow offshore areas, sandstones and shales nearer shore.

Although facies within the Grand Canyon are complex and numerous, they have been studied closely and described for more than a hundred years.

A few classic accounts of Grand Canyon geology are listed in the "To Read" section later in this chapter.

Defying the Law of Superposition. Sometimes we see older sedimentary rocks overlying younger rocks in the geologic record, often in situations where rocks have been folded intensely by mountain building and other crustal movement. In such cases, the orderly layering of rock has been disturbed so that time sequences are mixed up. In rare cases, older sedimentary rocks are found above younger rocks in situations in which no folding has occurred. If a limestone cave was submerged under the water in a lake or river, sand and silt would fill it, and burial of the cave under sediment could continue until the whole mass of sediments was deep underground undergoing compression and compaction. Millions of years later, after overlying material was stripped away, the cave limestones might be found to overlie a tube-shaped deposit of sandstone. Anyone encountering the sedimentary rocks may not know their ages, but the sequence of sedimentation might still be reasoned through and understood correctly. Then the observer might guess the relative ages of the sediments.

Another example might be found in the bed of a shifting river. Suppose a layer of hard sandstone formed an overhanging bank under which the river deposited silt. If the river continued depositing sediment in the area, as rivers do, the older sandstone deposits and underlying silt would be buried. Eventually the sediments would compact, and the rocks could be preserved as older sandstone (the overhanging bank) over younger siltstone (the deposited silt).

TO READ

Gilluly, James, Aaron C. Waters, and A. O. Woodford. *Principles of Geology.* San Francisco: W. H. Freeman and Company, 1975. Classic textbook with clear descriptions and excellent illustrations of sedimentary and other geological processes.

Leopold, Luna B. *A View of the River.* Cambridge, MA: Harvard University Press, 1994. Observations of major rivers of the world and how they function as great sediment transporters.

———. "The Rapids and Pools—Grand Canyon." In *The Colorado River Region and John Wesley Powell.* United States Geological Survey Professional Paper 669-C, 131–145. Washington, D.C.: U.S. Government Printing Office, 1969. Classic account of Colorado River dynamics in the Grand Canyon.

McKee, Edwin D. "Stratified Rocks of the Grand Canyon." In *The Colorado River Region and John Wesley Powell.* United States Geological Survey Professional Paper 669-B, 23–58. Washington, D.C.: U.S. Government Printing Office, 1969. McKee has studied rocks of the Grand Canyon extensively; this paper is considered definitive.

Powell, John Wesley. *The Exploration of the Colorado River and Its Canyons.* New York: Dover Publications, 1961. An account of the first two scientific expeditions by boat through the Grand Canyon by the man who named many of the canyon's sedimentary rocks.

TO WATCH

The Faces of Yellowstone. Dave Drum Associates, 1983. This videotape, shown at the visitors center in Yellowstone National Park, describes many of its hot-water mineral deposits.

How Do You Know? Collect the Data. Children's Television Workshop, 1991. A coral reef and the parrot fish it supports are examined closely.

The Making of a Continent: The Great River. Discovery Channel Signature Series. Discovery Channel, 1996. This videotape examines how human containment of the Mississippi River behind levees has caused changes in sediment deposition and shifts in the delta.

The Mississippi Delta. American Association of Petroleum Geologists–United States Geological Survey, 1985. This videotape shows many parts of a river system, including tributaries, river valleys, and deltas.

1923 Surveying Expedition of the Colorado River in Arizona. United States Geological Survey, 1973. This videotape includes the survey's 1923 movie footage of the Grand Canyon and the Colorado River.

Rapids of the Colorado River, Grand Canyon, Arizona. Open File Report 86-503. United States Geological Survey, 1986. Rapids on the Colorado River are shown, along with observed changes in the river.

CHAPTER 5

Fossils: Ancient Life

For thousands of years, people studied footprints, bones, and shells in rocks and labeled them according to myth and fairy tale. Old tusks from elephants were once called unicorns' horns. Certain worn animal teeth named toadstones were believed to have been derived from dying toads, and were said to cure some diseases. The thick, curved shells of the oyster *Gryphaea* were called devil's toenails. Circular shells from ocean creatures were thought to be coiled snakes turned to stone by an enchantress. None of this conjecture later proved true; the fossil hunters were correct only in that their finds were the remains of creatures from past ages.

BURIED CREATURES

For any animal or plant to become a fossil, it must be buried by sand, silt, mud, or other sediments in a river, lake, pond, swamp, or other environment. Although many organisms die and decompose on the ground before burial,

At one time, fossil mammoth tusks were thought to be unicorn's horns, and fossils of the Jurassic-period oyster were said to be toenails of the devil.

Fossil ammonites, such as this Jurassic-age Hildoceras, were believed to be coiled snakes turned to stone by an enchantress. Craftspeople sometimes carved snake heads on the ammonites to complete the image.

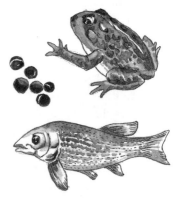

Toadstones, thought to be coughed up by toads, are actually the fossils of the powerful crushing teeth of the heavily scaled Jurassic-age fish, Lepidotus.

others are covered first and protected from rotting. Burial is most likely to occur underwater, where currents can quickly move sediment over dead creatures. Land organisms can be covered by windblown sand, volcanic ash, river muds, or natural tar. If a plant or animal is buried soon after its death, its bony or wooden hard parts—bones, shells, teeth, branches—may be preserved in the enclosing sediments.

Body parts can be preserved in several ways. Burial may be quick enough or the organism's environment so hot and dry that a body is preserved nearly intact, both in its chemical composition and structure. Or the hard parts may petrify (turn to stone) when rainwater seeps into microscopic pores throughout the bone or wood, leaching away the original material and filling the tiny holes with harder minerals. Fossils also are preserved when a creature's body parts dissolve away completely after burial, leaving behind an empty mold in the rock. If the mold later fills with mineral matter carried by seeping rainwater, a fossil cast is made.

Death, burial, and discovery: A fish dies and drifts to the seafloor, where it is quickly covered by the mud and silt moved by ocean currents. Its body decomposes, leaving only the hard bones, which are replaced over time by harder minerals carried by water that seeps through the sediment. More layers of sediment bury the fossil skeleton further. Over millions of years, the earth's surface changes and the sea ebbs, leaving the rocks on dry land. Millions of years of erosion may strip back the rocks, exposing the bones well enough for humans to find and excavate.

varieties of trace fossils

worm tracks crossing ripple marks made by waves of water over sand

worm burrows that churned up mud at the seashore

footprints of a three-toed dinosaur

dinosaur footprints and tailprint in the making

One way the soft parts of a creature may be fossilized: an insect is sealed in amber, the fossil sap from an ancient tree, from about 40 million years ago.

The petrified remains of plants and animals are common in the fossil record, but other types of fossils are important too. Trace fossils, which are just the clues left behind by animals, include burrows, tracks, footprints, eggs and shells, nests, and droppings.

An organism may leave behind only a trace of its existence. Trace fossils are preserved signs or trails, such as ancient footprints, gouges left by dragging animal tails, burrows made by worms, remains of eggs and shells, animal nests, and animal droppings. Or the traces may be of human activity, artifacts such as ancient stone tools or weapons, sometimes found with animal fossils.

Fossils known as inclusions are objects trapped in the hardened sap, or amber, of ancient evergreen trees. The inclusions may be insects, spiders, small lizards, and tiny bits of plants, preserved in perfect detail.

EARLY FINDS

The history of fossil study has been long and varied. Although speculation about fossils dates back thousands of years to the inquisitive Greeks, modern paleontology—the study of ancient life—began closer to the 1600s. In 1667, Nicholas Steno (the Danish physician from chapter 4), became fascinated with

William Smith, a leader in British geologic discovery, realized that rock layers, or strata, can be identified by the fossils they contain.

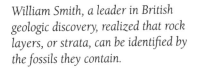

An engineer and surveyor, Smith prepared the first useful geologic maps from his journal notes on fossils and strata observed all over England.

small, sharp stones, popularly known as tongue stones, in larger beds of rock on the Mediterranean island of Malta. Steno applied his knowledge of anatomy to conclude that the tongue stones were ancient shark's teeth. He suggested that Malta must once have been under the sea, and the rocks that held the shark's teeth had been deposited by ocean water over a long period of time. He thereby became the first known scientist to document fossils as the remains of long-dead creatures—a foundational principle of paleontological study. From observations during his many geologic excursions, Steno also formulated Steno's laws—the law of superposition and the law of original horizontality—principles crucial to the understanding of rock deposition.

Scientists after Steno added observations to the growing science of paleontology. British land surveyor William Smith, while examining layers of rock for a coal-mining project in the early 1800s, noticed identical groups of fossils in similar rocks across England. He illustrated the fossils and their enclosing rock units, concluding that rocks containing like fossils must be of the same age, wherever they are found in the world.

The work of Steno, Smith, and others of equal importance indicated that fossils must be approximately the same age as the rocks that hold them. Younger rocks therefore enclose younger fossils than older rocks. And unless rocks have been overturned or bent by crustal folding, layers of younger rocks, with their younger fossils, overlie older layers of both.

FIRST FOSSILS

The oldest known fossils, which date back to 3.5 billion years ago, are collections of algae. Scientists believe that the sun's rays heating the earth's first oceans created ideal conditions for the growth of proteins, chains of complex chemicals, in seawater. Over time, these simple life forms changed, or evolved, into more complicated forms: single-celled, bacterialike algae. As they died, they fell and piled up in huge mats on the ocean floors. When fossilized, they formed huge beds of limestone and stromatolites, mounds of layered blue-green algae that look like cabbages made of rock. Extensive deposits of stromatolites were found in Canada in the Gunflint Chert, 2-billion-year-old, ocean-deposited rocks.

The early atmosphere of the planet had no oxygen, and the blue-green algae that made up the stromatolites needed no oxygen to survive. But as they took energy from the sun, they digested their own food and gave off oxygen as waste. After thousands of years of countless algae constantly producing oxygen, the earth's atmosphere changed in composition. By 1.5 billion years ago, larger, more complex animals evolved and thrived in the presence of

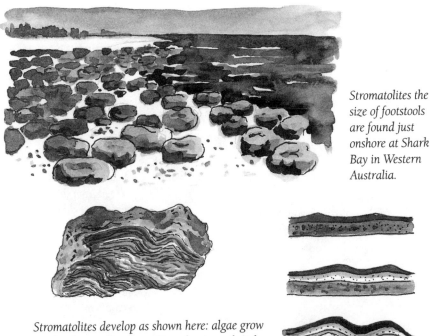

Stromatolites the size of footstools are found just onshore at Shark Bay in Western Australia.

Stromatolites develop as shown here: algae grow on mud; a layer of mud or silt washes in and sticks to the algae, allowing new algae to grow on top; more layers alternate and heap up in mounds.

oxygen. Fossil finds in sedimentary deposits in the Ediacara Hills of Australia turned up well-preserved evidence of soft-bodied ocean animals from 670 million years ago: jellyfish, sea pens (which resemble ferns), and arthropods (ancestors of today's crabs, lobsters, and insects).

SHELLS AND BACKBONES

The first creatures of the ancient seas had no backbones, teeth, or other easily preserved parts to contribute to the fossil record, but that changed when hard-shelled creatures entered the picture 570 million years ago. Rocks deposited since that time contain abundant fossils, because more hard parts were available to preserve. Animals probably developed shells because of a change in environment—perhaps the acidity of the sea changed. Oceans came alive with brachiopods (clamlike creatures), graptolites (wormlike animals in branched colonies), trilobites (animals with outer skeletons and jointed legs), coral, jellyfish, sea sponges, and sea anemones. Some primitive fishes developed backbones. Fossils from around 500 million years ago show that early fishes had bony plates covering their heads, rows of scales on their sides, and no fins or jaws.

A fossil brachiopod (lamp shell) from the Pennsylvanian period is shown embedded in limestone.

A similar brachiopod has eroded from the limestone that once held it.

A section of the stem of a fossil crinoid, or Pennsylvanian-age "sea lily," is shown as it once lived, attached by its stem to the ocean floor.

Soft-bodied creatures lived on as well, developing adaptations to changes in the oceans. Although the soft-bodied survivors still left few remains in the fossil record, an important 530-million-year-old fossil deposit in Canada, the Burgess Shale, provides a glimpse of the wide variety of shapes assumed by soft-bodied creatures in those early years. Their bodies were preserved in amazing detail in the fine-grained shales, thought to have been deposited by ocean currents spilling over into nearby lagoons.

Between 400 and 350 million years ago, oxygen in the atmosphere, which had been building gradually since life began on earth, became abundant enough to ring the planet in a layer of ozone, much as it is today. Living things could survive out of water, protected from the sun by the ozone. Over many millions of years, as life still flourished in the oceans, some mosslike sea plants washed up onto land and took root, to become the first creatures to live on shore. As early as 395 million years ago, amphibians evolved from developing fishes, growing lungs that enabled them to live for short periods out of water: Extensive deposits of 380-million-year-old Old Red Sandstone in Scotland and in the United States (in New York, Pennsylvania, and West Virginia) contain fossils of lobe-fin fishes, creatures with both fish and amphibian characteristics—fish scales as well as strong-boned, lobe-shaped fins that later evolved into feet.

A GREAT EXTINCTION

From 350 to 250 million years ago, forests of horsetails, ferns, and cone-bearing trees spread over the land. Reptiles colonized areas farther inland than amphibians could with their more primitive lungs. Reptiles also dominated the seas and air by evolving both swimming and flying forms. Rocks deposited in the rivers, swamps, lakes, and oceans of 300 million years ago are rich in fossils of ancient reptiles, fishes, woody plants, mollusks (shellfish), coral, horsetails, land snails, centipedes, millipedes, and cockroaches.

The fossil record of 225 million years ago, however, shows a big break in evolutionary lines. More than 90 percent of all plant and animal species died out in an extinction even larger than that of the dinosaurs 180 million years later. Many scientists believe that the mass extinction of 225 million years ago, a time of crisis for global life, was due to a gradual drying of the earth's shallow seas. The shrinking of the oceans left fewer places for plants and animals to survive. Half the species of jellyfishes, sponges, mollusks, worms, and fishes were wiped out. Only four of fifteen major groups of reptiles survived. Trilobites did not survive, nor did horned corals and many brachiopods. Overall, only about five of every hundred species remained. All life on the planet today evolved from the few survivors of that great extinction, filling empty niches in new ways.

Some ocean reptiles survived, responding to the great drying of the oceans by once again moving onto land. These new land reptiles looked somewhat like modern crocodiles—great lizardlike creatures with muscular hind legs. They also had distinctive hip joints that would eventually allow them to walk upright—as ancestral dinosaurs.

THE DINOSAURS

In 1822, British fossil collector Mary Ann Mantell, searching a roadway under repair, found a fossil bone that looked like a huge stone tooth. Further searching nearby revealed associated bones resembling those of the reptile iguana, only sixty times the size. Scientists who studied Mantell's find named it Iguanodon (meaning iguana tooth), observing that it no longer existed on earth. In subsequent years, fossil hunting around the world turned up fossils of other large, extinct reptiles that had a curious difference from today's reptiles. The extinct creatures apparently had walked with their feet set beneath them. Reptiles today walk with a wide, splayed-out stance. On the basis of this fossil evidence, scientists found it necessary to name a new family of animals. In 1841, Richard Owen, an anatomist at the London Natural History Museum, proposed the name dinosauria, meaning "terrible lizards," for the ancient reptiles.

In their time, dinosaurs achieved great diversity, ruling the world for 160 million years. The fossil evidence indicates abundant shapes and abilities: Some dinosaurs had long necks for browsing treetops like giraffes, some were meat eaters that could chase their prey at high speeds, some had wings and presumbly could fly. Hundreds of species of dinosaurs have been discovered around the world, and some paleontologists believe that thousands more will be found over time.

For all their marvelous adaptations and success as a family, dinosaurs disappeared from the fossil record beginning in rocks approximately 65 million years old. Some scientists believe that a gradual climate change brought about the mass extinction. Others theorize that a global catastrophe such as a meteor collision with the earth or widespread volcanic eruptions caused the mass disappearance. Still others believe that some deadly disease spread throughout

Mary Ann Mantell, a fossil collector by hobby, found remains of the dinosaur Iguanodon *in rocks dug up during road construction.*

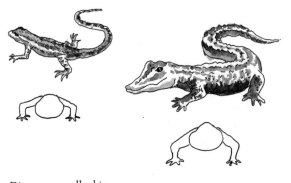

*Dinosaurs walked in
a stance that improved upon
that of other tetrapods, or four-legged animals.
Reptiles such as lizards sprawl, their legs out to the side.
Crocodiles can rise when needed and hurry along with bodies
high above the ground. But dinosaurs had legs like pillars, supporting their bodies from
directly underneath, much like horses. Dinosaurs therefore were more efficient than either
lizards or crocodiles at running and supporting their heavy body weights.*

the world, carried from continent to continent by the wandering dinosaurs themselves. Whatever the cause, because the dinosaurs died out, other species of animals were able to flourish.

BEYOND THE DINOSAURS

While dinosaurs ruled the earth, other plants and animals thrived as well in the mild, moist climates that covered the land. Plants evolved rapidly, including ferns, ginkgo (maidenhair) trees, cone-bearing trees, and cycads (palm-like tropical plants). Flowering plants developed toward the end of the time of dinosaurs, providing them and other land creatures with a quickly repro-ducing and spreading food source. In the oceans, species such as ammonoids, oysters, and brachiopods evolved and dispersed widely. Large, meat-eating plesiosaurs and icthyosaurs, swimming reptiles not considered to be dino-saurs, ruled the oceans. Pterosaurs, winged reptiles that gradually evolved to the size of today's small airplanes, took to the air. Other reptiles—crocodiles, turtles, and lizards—also spread and left abundant fossils in rocks approxi-mately 200 to 65 million years old.

The first birds developed during the dinosaur era, as was discovered in the Solnhofen limestone in Germany, a 140-million-year-old limestone fine grained enough to preserve detailed impressions of fossil crayfish, jellyfish,

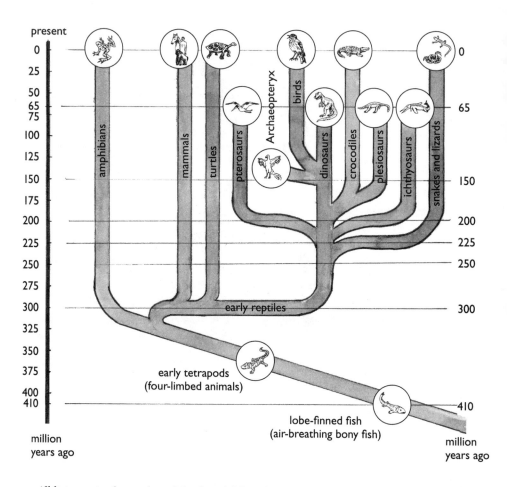

All living animals may have lobe-finned fish and early tetrapods as their common ancestors, as this drawing shows. Dinosaurs and other well-known creatures branched off from early reptiles at varying times in response to environmental changes. Some animal species survived until today; many did not.

pterosaurs, insects, and dinosaurs. Among these impressions of delicate features in the Solnhofen deposits are the world's oldest known fossilized feathers, associated with a crow-sized bird, *Archaeopteryx,* which also had teeth and clawed wings—reptilian characteristics.

One group of land animals living during the reign of the dinosaurs survived by maintaining small sizes, hiding from the great reptiles, eating insects, and foraging mostly at night. When the dinosaurs and large reptiles were wiped out 65 million years ago, these small, adaptive creatures—mammals—

lived on with the smaller reptiles (crocodiles, snakes, lizards, and turtles), amphibians, bony fishes, and birds. Over the next 60 million years, modern life forms diversified from early mammalian rodents and primates (apes and monkeys), as well as large flightless birds, flowering plants, fishes, sharks, and sea clams and snails.

Fifty-million-year-old fossils provide glimpses of life forms that survived and developed after the dinosaur-age extinction. Preserved horse's teeth and foot bones show that early horses were short, five-toed creatures that gradually, over millions of years, increased in size and developed the faster, tougher hoof of the modern horse. Fossils of early barnacles, sea urchins, sea snails, and whales show that their shells and skeletons changed over time—for example, sea urchins took on many shapes and ancient whales gradually acquired teeth. Fossils of early tree species suggest that they became more rare as flowering grasses spread, replacing forests in many areas. Fossils of animals that roamed the new grasslands indicate great herds of grazing animals, such as pigs, camels, rhinos, antelopes, and horses. Fossil apes are common in European and African rocks of 25 million years ago. And fossils of humanlike primates date back to 10 to 20 million years ago.

THE HUMAN RECORD

We have known of fossil humans only for about one hundred years. By the 1880s, only a few specimens of fossil humans had been found in Africa and Asia. Today, anthropologists, scientists who study human fossils, work at sites all over the world. Discoveries of human fossils are more common as searches become more intensive, and each discovery raises new questions about the human family tree.

The puzzle of human evolution is not complete, because fossils are rare overall and provide only pieces of information on how we began. The oldest humanlike bones were found in Ethiopia, Africa, in the early 1970s, in an excavation of at least fourteen individual early humans known to scientists as The First Family. There, the bones of a 4-million-year-old female, named Lucy by scientists, showed that she walked upright, had hands and feet like humans, left footprints much like humans, but had a brain about one-fourth the size of ours.

Scientists have found enough specimens to reason that Lucy's ancestral line died out more than 1 million years ago. Human fossils from later years, the remains of a family line named *Homo* (man), show a larger brain size, approximately the same as we have today. *Homo erectus,* our large-brained, upright-walking, immediate forebears, could stand and search the growing grasslands for the animals they hunted. They could carry food home in their arms to growing communities of families and could fashion tools and scrape hides for clothing. They lived well enough off the meat of the huge beasts of their day—woolly mammoths, saber-toothed tigers, giant wolves, and sloths—to follow them in their migrations to all the continents of the world. Their intelligence, combined with the physical changes that came with an upright stance, remained as the line evolved into *Homo sapiens,* the species of human that survives to this day.

TO DO

FOSSIL HUNTING

What you will need

hand lens

notebook

rock hammer (optional)

sun hat

layers of clothing

outdoor shoes or boots

pocket guide to fossils

compass

location and geologic maps

Searching for fossils requires little more than the proper field equipment and comfortable clothing.

First identify your area of interest and decide where you want to go. Do you want to look at fossils of ancient shelled creatures, dinosaurs, or fernlike plants? Are you interested in a particular geologic time, such as the time of the woolly mammoths and other big mammals or the time when trilobites filled the seas? Check your pocket guide for the age of fossils that interest you and the types of rock they are usually found in. Also check your local library, museums, and bookstores. Often fossil specimens can be found near your home, if you know details about them before you set out. Compare the information you uncover from the above resources with a geologic map of your area.

If you decide to fossil hunt on privately owned land, you must get permission from the landowner by telephoning or sending a letter. Even if the area is publicly owned, you need permission from the organization in charge if you plan to do more than look, draw, or photograph.

Once in the field, look for biological forms: ring shapes of shells, branching patterns of plants, cylindrical shapes of long shells, subtle imprints of feet, or animal burrows. Sketch what you find in your notebook, and pay close attention to the rocks as well as their fossils.

Explanation: Rocks proven to contain fossils in the past may hold many more, still undiscovered. You have only to spot them. Charles Walcott, the man who discovered the famous soft-bodied creatures of the Burgess Shale, simply chanced upon them. He had just spent weeks collecting trilobites in nearby locations and was headed home. The trail out of his field location happened to pass by shales rich in previously undiscovered fossils.

Remember that guidelines for finding fossils are only guidelines. Stay open-minded about what you might see in the field. Observe, take notes, and think.

MODELING GEOLOGIC TIME

What you will need

a long sheet of paper

a geology reference book

pens (many colors will help)

ruler

Drawing a model of geologic time will help you grasp the concept of millions and billions of years.

Draw a 5-foot (1.5 meter) horizontal line across the bottom of a long sheet of paper taken from a roll or made of taped sheets. Mark the endpoints of the line with vertical marks. Label the left endpoint as the Precambrian Era (time of early life; 4.6 billion to 570 million years ago). Label the right endpoint as the Cenozoic Era (time of common life; 65 million years ago to the present). Divide the line into increments of one inch (2.5 centimeters). The first billions of years of life on earth—the first nine-tenths of all earth's lifetime—left few fossils, so you can condense the Precambrian Era into three of the increments and use the remaining fifty-seven to represent the next 570 million years.

Mark the Paleozoic Era (time of ancient life; 570 to 245 million years ago) and the Mesozoic Era (245 to 65 million years ago) in the appropriate places on your time line. Write in the geologic highlights and add fossil names and ages.

Next, mark the divisions on your chart for the periods, which are subdivisions of the eras. (Note that the Precambrian Era is not subdivided into periods.) Use different pen colors if desired for clarity.

Paleozoic Era:	Cambrian Period	570 to 505 million years ago
	Ordovician Period	505 to 438 million years ago
	Silurian Period	438 to 408 million years ago
	Devonian Period	408 to 360 million years ago
	Mississippian Period	360 to 320 million years ago
	Pennsylvanian Period	320 to 286 million years ago
	Permian Period	286 to 225 million years ago
Mesozoic Era:	Triassic Period	225 to 208 million years ago
	Jurassic Period	208 to 144 million years ago
	Cretaceous Period	144 to 65 million years ago
Cenozoic Era:	Tertiary Period	65 to 1.5 million years ago
	Quaternary Period	1.5 million years ago to present

Now fill in the time slots with the names of fossils from this chapter. Write and sketch in stromatolites, trilobites, brachiopods, large swimming reptiles, the first amphibians, dinosaurs, grasslands, and the first humans. For more information, check your geology reference books.

Explanation: Locating important fossils in time will help you understand how geologists defined the eras and periods of the vast span of geologic time. Because known fossils are rare in the Precambrian Era, that time is not subdivided into periods on the basis of fossil evidence. Scientists did subdivide the other eras, however, according to the many shelled and hard-bodied creatures that developed and evolved from around 570 years ago.

The names of the eras and periods are connected with the life forms of the times. Mesozoic means "middle life." The Jurassic Period was named for the Jura Mountains of Switzerland after fossils of that time period were found in those mountains. The Pennsylvanian and Mississippian periods were similarly named, although these names are used only in the United States. Consult your geology references for more information.

MOVING BONES

What you will need

a handful of round toothpicks

notebook

Fossil bones may not lie in the positions they assumed when the animal died. This experiment shows why.

Find a flat, smooth surface outdoors, exposed to wind and precipitation. Set five or six toothpicks in an orderly pattern on the surface. Sketch the pattern in your field notebook. Note the time of day, weather, and wind direction. If you have pets that might disturb the toothpicks, good. Chance encounters with animals are part of the experiment. Leave the toothpicks alone, but check them occasionally. Note the times and any changes in weather. If the toothpicks have moved, sketch a picture in your notebook and note what caused them to move. After several days, draw a final picture of their pattern. Check to see how the pattern relates to prevailing wind or other environmental factors.

Explanation: What happens to an organism between its time of death and time of burial affects how its fossils will appear. In this experiment, the toothpicks represent fossil bones, which may be carried off by scavenging animals, roll on the bottom of a river, scatter in ocean currents, sweep away in floods, or decompose before burial. As they are rearranged, the bones often bunch into little groups, pushed by the wind or water currents. If they were real fossils, they might next be buried by blowing sand or water-carried sediment.

LOOKING FOR FOSSIL TRACKS

What you will need

hand lens

notebook

binoculars

Animal tracks provide clues about how they may become trace fossils in the future.

As you go on hikes—in the woods, in parks, at the beach, in empty lots near your home—look for animals and their footprints. You may see an animal and then snoop around to find its tracks, or you can check the edges of puddles or ponds. When you find some animal tracks, sketch them and identify them from guidebooks (see "To Read" later in this chapter). Think about the tales the tracks tell. How wet was the mud when the tracks were made? Is it still that wet? How long ago do you think the animals came for water? How many different types of animals visited? Will the tracks eventually become fossils?

Explanation: To become a fossil track, a footprint must be made in sediment that can take and hold an impression. The mud, sand, or silt should be moderately wet. If the sediments are dry, they may not be soft enough to imprint or they may blow away in the wind. The footprint must also be buried quickly, before it can crumble, to become a fossil. Most fossil footprints were probably made near or in water, where sediment quickly washed in to fill them.

Tracks tell us about an animal's habits—where it goes for food, where it sleeps, whether it travels in groups. Walking animals leave full prints, complete from heel to toe. Running animals often leave deeper toe prints than heel prints. The distance between footprints—an animal's stride—is important in estimating how quickly the animal was moving when it made the tracks. Scientists have been able to measure the stride indicated by some dinosaur footprints to calculate the animals' rate of speed. Some sauropods, like brachiosaurus, moved like elephants, with a top speed of about 16 miles (26 kilometers) per hour. Triceratops may have moved more like rhino, running at 20 miles (32 kilometers) per hour. Three-toed dinosaurs, about the size of ostriches, trotted at 11 miles (18 kilometers) per hour and could dash up to 25 miles (40 kilometers) per hour.

MAKING MOLDS AND CASTS OF TRACKS

What you will need

plaster of paris

water

plastic container for mixing in

clean cardboard milk carton

masking tape

large spoon

pocketknife

liquid dish soap

Fossil tracks can be found in rock as molds and casts. You can make both using plaster of paris.

Find a footprint to cast. Following the directions on the package, mix the plaster of paris in the plastic container. Spoon the mixed plaster in a layer about 1 inch (2.5 centimeters) thick over the footprint. Let the mixture set for a few hours, until it is pretty hard. Then you can remove it from the ground and take it indoors overnight to harden completely. You will then have a cast of the footprint.

In the morning, brush the cast clean. Using your pocketknife to remove extra plaster, trim the cast to the size of the milk carton—cut in half to make a 4-inch (10-centimeter) high container—and set the cast inside, footprint side up. Coat the top of the cast with a generous layer of dish soap. Let the soap seep down all along the sides of the cast.

Next, mix another batch of plaster. Spoon it in over the top of the cast. Let the mixture harden all day and overnight. The next morning, tear away the milk carton and see what has happened. You should be able to pull apart the two halves—both cast and mold—of your plaster creation.

Explanation: Animals leave footprints that sometimes act as molds, filling with soil and sand that eventually harden into rocks. In this experiment, the original filling hardens into a cast. When the finished cast is set inside the milk carton and covered with plaster, the result is a mold that should closely resemble the original footprint.

TO THINK ABOUT

Fierce Hunting Machines. In his book *Wild to the Heart,* Rick Bass wrote about U.S. Forest Service employees who look for and count grizzly bears in Wyoming. One of the men, Wayne Jenkins, had not seen a grizzly bear on the job since his first year out:

> Jenkins has seen a wild bear up here once in seventeen years—coincidentally, seventeen years ago, his first year on this job—and she was on a streamside, a long way off, in the morning sun . . . flipping over boulders with one paw, boulders that three or four strong men wouldn't ever be able to budge . . . . Wayne and his father, who was eighty then, watched the mother [bear] move all the way down the streamside and into the woods; the meadow looked afterward as if it had been mined: boulders strewn, some having tumbled all the way down into the stream. The sun on her long claws. Wayne said he was a hundred yards away, up in the trees, on a ledge, and was terrified.

Grizzly bears are huge, powerful animals. They can run 30 miles (50 kilometers) an hour. *Tyrannosaurus rex,* the largest and fiercest meateater of all time, grew to be as big as a large building and had teeth as long as your forearm. It could run 50 miles (80 kilometers) an hour in pursuit of prey. Imagine being in the same time zone as a live *Tyrannosaurus rex.* How far apart would you have to be not to feel terrified?

Natural Selection. In the 1850s, a scientist named Charles Darwin wrote a book called *On the Origin of Species by Means of Natural Selection, or the Preservation of Favoured Races in the Struggle for Life.* The book was one of the first to describe how evolution works through changes in plants or animals over time. Darwin pointed out that most living things produce many more offspring than will survive. For example, a female frog may lay several thousand eggs. Because of environmental factors, such as small food supplies, cold, or drought, only dozens of the frogs may survive. Only the strongest offspring tend to live through tough times, a fact that Darwin called survival of the fittest. Because the fit survive, they can have offspring, which also tend to be strong and fit. Darwin wrote about and presented his ideas only after many years of study and countless miles of gathering information all over the world. His theory of survival and evolution, called natural selection, is now widely accepted as being true.

Scientists now believe that all life on earth evolved from the first proteins in the primeval oceans on our planet. Evolutionary changes from these original life forms came gradually in response to environmental factors. Darwin found evidence for such adaptive changes by observing the characteristics of thirteen closely-related species of finches on the Galápagos islands in South America. He theorized that the world retains the original life form as well as gaining the new, resulting in more diversity in species on the planet.

Warm- or Cold-Blooded? For many years, scientists believed that dinosaurs were cold-blooded reptiles, relying on surrounding environmental temperatures for warming and cooling. Current thought is that at least some species of dinosaurs were warm-blooded, maintaining internal body temperatures by eating food for fuel. Warm-blooded animals, such as humans, take in large amounts of food. We depend on our hearts to pump heated blood throughout our bodies and so keep our body temperatures relatively high and constant. *Tyrannosaurus rex* had a huge rib cage and chest area that probably accommodated a strong, warm-blooded heart. It also had powerful leg bones and muscles to hunt quickly and ferociously for the vast amounts of food it needed to survive.

Darwin's observation of adaptation in finches

The small ground finch eats small, soft seeds.

The woodpecker finch uses its specialized beak to break off a cactus spine, which it uses as a probing tool for finding wood-boring insects.

The medium ground finch, with its heavier beak, can manage both small, soft seeds and some larger, harder seeds.

The cactus finch and large cactus finch have sharp beaks well adapted to eating cactus fruits and flowers.

A larger, stronger beak allows the large ground finch to crack and eat the toughest seeds.

Charles Darwin observed thirteen different species of finches on the Galápagos Islands, off the coast of Ecuador, South America. As he watched the birds, Darwin came to believe that the various finches descended from a single finch species, each evolving with a beak specialized for a particular type of food gathering. This led him to conclude that species of plants and animals evolve and change as they adapt to their environments. This drawing shows six of Darwin's finches.

Another dinosaur, triceratops, probably moved as powerfully as a bull and fought off predators with its three-horned snout and forehead. Triceratops lived in herds that may have migrated long distances with changing seasons. Some paleontologists believe that the migrating dinosaurs must have been warm-blooded to maintain energy on long trips, like warm-blooded caribou that go where food is available in winter.

Any warm-blooded animal population has small numbers of large, meat-eating predators compared with the larger numbers of grazing prey, such as on the African savanna, where lions are much fewer than gazelles. Fossil dinosaur bone sites usually contain 1 to 3 percent predators such as tyrannosaurus and 97 to 99 percent grazers such as stegosaurus or diplodocus. Such evidence is compelling in favor of some warm-bloodedness among the dinosaurs, although the jury remains out in the great debate.

TO READ

Benton, Michael. *The Story of Life on Earth: Tracing Its Origins and Development through Time.* New York: Warwich Press, 1986. An indispensable resource on the evolution of life through the ages; well illustrated and complete.

Bradbury, Ray. *Dinosaur Tales.* New York: Bantam Books, 1983. An illustrated collection of Bradbury's imaginative stories about dinosaurs.

Gould, Stephen J. *Wonderful Life: The Burgess Shale and the Nature of History.* New York: W. W. Norton and Company, 1989. The fascinating tale—with must-see illustrations—of interpreting the strange fossils in the Cambrian Burgess Shale.

Horner, John R., and Don Lessem. *Digging Up* Tyrannosaurus rex. New York: Crown Publishers, 1992. The well-told story of the discovery and excavation of a nearly complete *Tyrannosaurus rex* fossil.

Moorehead, Alan. *Darwin and the Beagle.* New York: Harper & Row, 1969. Fascinating account of Charles Darwin's scientific expedition to South America in the 1830s.

Murie, Olaus J. *A Field Guide to Animal Tracks.* Boston: Houghton Mifflin Company, 1954. A classic guide, essential to any search for tracks.

Parker, Steve, and Raymond L. Bernor, eds. *The Practical Paleontologist.* New York: Simon and Schuster—Fireside, 1990. A fun nuts-and-bolts approach to fossil hunting.

Ransom, Jay E. *Fossils in America: Their Nature, Origin, Identification, and Classification, and a Range Guide to Collecting Sites, 1964.* New York: Harper & Row, 1964. A good state-by-state resource for those who wish to collect fossils in the United States.

Rhodes, Frank H. T., Herbert S. Zim, and Paul R. Shaffer. *Fossils: A Guide to Prehistoric Life*. New York: Golden Press, 1962. A handy and comprehensive pocket guide for fossil hunting in the field.

Stegner, Wallace. *Mormon Country*. New York: Bonanza Books, 1962. Includes a chapter (*Notes on a Life Spent Pecking at a Sandstone Cliff*) about the work of Earl Douglass, who devoted his life to excavating dinosaur bones in northeastern Utah.

Stein, Sara. *The Evolution Book*. New York: Workman Publishing, 1986. The earth's outstanding evolutionary events described clearly and accompanied by hands-on activities.

Taylor, Paul D. *Fossil*. New York: Alfred A. Knopf, 1990. Color photographs show many different kinds of fossils, from bacteria and algae to birds and mammals.

TO WATCH

The Dinosaurs! PBS Home Videos, 1992. Part One: "The Monsters Emerge." Part Two: "Flesh on the Bones." Part Three: "The Nature of the Beast." Part Four: "The Death of the Dinosaurs." Facts and theories about dinosaurs, including interviews with distinguished paleontologists and films of fossil digs.

Lost Worlds, Vanished Lives. David Attenborough, 1989. Program One: "Magic in the Rocks." Program Two: "Putting Flesh on Bone." Program Three: "Dinosaurs." Program Four: "The Rare Glimpses." A good look at the history of paleontology, with film of many kinds of fossil digs all over the world.

Mammoths of the Ice Age, NOVA series. WGBH Educational Foundation, 1995. Recent theories on how long ago woolly mammoths died out, where they lived and migrated, and their habits and diet as revealed by fossil evidence.

CHAPTER 6

Erosion: Tearing Down Rocks

Geology is not all about depositing and creating rock. Many geologic processes are those of erosion, helping to shape the world's landscapes by breaking down rock physically or chemically and moving it elsewhere. In most environments, rock is both created and destroyed, often in separate areas. Beaches, for example, have areas of deposition, such as where streams lay down sediment near their mouths at the ocean, and areas of erosion, where currents move sand grains from the beach and down the coast or where repeated wave action breaks down the rocky cliffs at the sea's edge. Sometimes deposition dominates an environment, and sometimes erosion dominates. In any area where erosion dominates, losses of material outweigh gains—rock is broken down and moved elsewhere, but its loss is not balanced by the addition of more material. In this way, over time, landforms are leveled, and even the world's largest mountains are stripped away.

The type of erosion that occurs in any environment depends on what natural forces are at play. In a river environment the river may cut down into the surrounding rock, and the resulting debris is carried downstream by stream action. In a desert environment with little vegetation to protect sediments from high winds, wind erosion will certainly dominate. Erosion occurs in as many different ways as there are individual landscapes, but the processes that erode rock can be described generally as mass wasting, stream erosion, weathering, glacial activity, and wind action.

MASS WASTING

Landslides and other types of movement of loose rock and soil down hills and mountain slopes are known as mass wasting. The movement is not caused by the action of ice, wind, or water, although these forces can affect and help move rocks already involved in mass wasting. Instead, the main driver behind mass wasting is gravity, which pulls material down slopes in two quite different ways: through slope failure and sediment flows.

Slope Failure. When the rock or soil on a hillside slumps, falls, or slides in sudden releases, the movement is called slope failure. Slumps, falls, or slides may or may not display warning signs, such as breaks and bulges in a hillside before it gives way. In all slope failures, material is moved by gravity from the higher to the lower slopes.

In slumps, rock and soil break away beginning at the top of the slope, slipping down curved surfaces to create large, displaced blocks. Slumps occur most frequently at times of heavy rain or after sudden shocks like earthquakes, when the blocks are more easily dislodged for movement.

Falls, true to their name, are freefalls of material from hillsides. Pieces of bedrock or debris (rock mixed with sediment and plant material) break loose and fall through the air to surfaces below.

A slide, in contrast, is the movement of rock and debris directly down a slope's inclined surface. Slides are common on steep slopes in high mountains, where the material moves short or long distances depending on the length of the slope.

Sediment Flows. Sediment mixed with enough water can flow like water in a stream. When sediment and debris flow rather than falling, sliding, tumbling, or rolling, the movement of the material is called sediment flow. Sediment flows are either slurry flows, in which sediment mixed with water moves down the slope, or granular flows, in which sediment, air, and water mix to travel downslope.

In slurry flows, the mixture of sediment and water is extremely dense. Large boulders may be suspended (held up) by the flow, and boulders too large

three types of slope failure

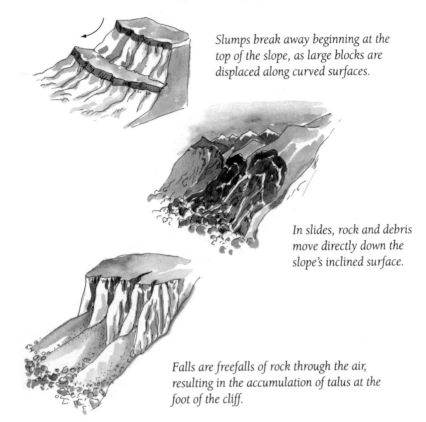

Slumps break away beginning at the top of the slope, as large blocks are displaced along curved surfaces.

In slides, rock and debris move directly down the slope's inclined surface.

Falls are freefalls of rock through the air, resulting in the accumulation of talus at the foot of the cliff.

to be suspended may roll along in it. Soil, rock, debris, and mud may all flow together, resulting in mixed and unsorted sediment moving downhill. Slurry flows are common on active volcanoes in wet climates. Layers of older volcanic debris can be set in motion by the rapid melting of snow and ice from new volcanic activity. Slurry flows consisting of mud, known as mudflows, are among the greatest hazards associated with volcanoes, creating some of the worst natural disasters in human history. When Mount Vesuvius erupted in 79 A.D., mudflows engulfed the Roman city of Herculaneum at approximately the same time falling ash covered the town of Pompeii. One of the most devastating mudflows on record destroyed the village of Armero in the Andes in Colombia, South America, in 1985. Mount St. Helens in Washington has produced many mudflows through its years of activity, most recently in May 1980, when mudflows traveled east and west of the mountain at speeds averaging 15 miles (25 kilometers) per hour and as high as 90 miles (145 kilometers) per

A mudflow is a mixture of sediment and water that easily flows downhill.

Earthflows are forms of granular flows, recognizable by stepped slopes fringed by rounded accumulations of earth at the bottom, or toe.

toe

hour. Several spectators hoping to see the eruption of St. Helens from a safe distance were trapped and buried by the mudflows.

In contrast to wet, saturated slurry flows, granular flows may contain large amounts of air or hold such a wide variety of particle shapes and sizes that water can escape easily from between them. Debris avalanches and earthflows are examples of granular flows.

Avalanches of rock and debris are the best-known types of granular flow, in which material falls, breaks apart on impact with the ground surface, and continues down the slope. Avalanches pose the greatest threat to human life in mountainous areas such as the European Alps and South American Andes, which have centers of population scattered throughout their high valleys. One famous avalanche occurred on Mont Blanc, in the French-Italian Alps, in 1717, when an avalanche of rock and ice covered two villages and all their inhabitants, who could not have escaped in the two to four minutes it took the avalanche to travel 4.5 miles (7 kilometers).

Other granular flows take the form of earthflows. Earthflows are common on hillsides, identified by their long tongue shapes and their rounded, bulging downhill edges, called toes. In an earthflow, an entire piece of slope moves, often after a period of heavy rainfall. One special type of earthflow occurs in wet clay or sand made weak by shaking, such as that of an earthquake. The shaking causes liquefaction, a process whereby the sediment acts as a fluid.

STREAM EROSION

Water is a great transporter of sediment over the face of continents. Even before they join with other drops of water into streams, raindrops fall from the sky, hit the ground, and displace particles of soil from the land. Together, the drops become sheets of water traveling over land, moving toward streams and rivers that lead to the ocean. In the streams, the sediment becomes part of the stream's load (the particles the stream carries), as its bed load, suspended load, or dissolved load.

Large particles of sediment move along the bottom of the streambed, sliding and rolling more slowly than water in the stream. These particles are the stream's bed load. Sometimes the stream's energy, or amount and speed of water flow, is great enough to lift pieces of the bed load from the bottom. If so, they make short jumps above the streambed, still working downstream. A stream can move its bed load in times of swifter flow and in its higher-energy reaches, but during times of waning flow or in calm stretches of the river, sediment that could move as part of the bed load will remain on the streambed.

Finer particles are carried as bits of sediment held up, or suspended, in

stream erosion

Small particles of sediment are held in suspension in the water as the stream's suspended load.

Large particles of sediment—cobbles and boulders— move along the bottom as the stream's bed load.

A cross section of a stream showing how its load is distributed.

stream water. Great amounts of sediment are moved by suspension in rivers. Many rivers take their colors and names from the types of sediment they carry. China's Huang He, or Yellow River, carries large amounts of yellowish silt transported from land throughout its drainage basin. Arizona's Colorado River—Spanish for red—turns the color of old brick when its tributaries swell with water and bits of red rock eroded from upstream areas by rain and wind.

Even clear streams carry eroded material: chemical substances that have dissolved from surrounding rock and other sources. Bicarbonate, calcium, sulfate, chloride, sodium, magnesium, and potassium are dissolved and carried by the water of most rivers.

Eventually the particles and chemicals eroded from the land by fresh water in a stream travel to the sea to become sediment deposited in ocean environments.

WEATHERING

Any rock that is exposed to the earth's atmosphere is subject to weathering, or breakdown and change through chemical or mechanical processes. In chemical weathering, rocks and minerals decompose through the work of chemical reactions upon their molecular structures. In mechanical weathering, rocks disintegrate by physically breaking up into pieces.

Chemical Weathering. The minerals in igneous and metamorphic rocks, created within the earth, are subject to change when brought to the surface and exposed to the atmosphere. Much of this change occurs through the work of water, which picks up chemicals as it falls as rain through the air or percolates through soil. The main chemical it picks up is carbon dioxide—a chemical with molecules made of one carbon atom and two oxygen atoms—which when dissolved in water becomes carbonic acid, a weak acid rich in hydrogen atoms. The acid, working on the surface of a rock or through its cracks or fractures, can change the chemical composition of the rock's minerals. The changes occur when carbonic acid actually replaces some of the atoms in a mineral with atoms of its own. Granite, for example, generally rich in the minerals quartz, mica, and feldspar, will weather gradually to clay by trading sodium and potassium atoms for the hydrogen atoms in carbonic acid. The quartz will remain largely unaltered, but the feldspar and mica will weather to clay minerals. Similarly, the minerals in basalt will weather to clay by trading their sodium, calcium, and magnesium atoms for carbonic acid's hydrogens.

Water is not the only substance that can cause chemical weathering in a rock. The presence of oxygen can set off chemical reactions as well, by exchanging its atoms with those of the minerals it touches in a process known as oxidation. Iron, a common element in many minerals, changes its form and color through oxidation. In taking on extra oxygen atoms, the iron becomes the clay mineral goethite. In turn, goethite may alter, often by losing water molecules from its mineral structure, to hematite, an important mineral ore for iron. Hematite in its altered form is reddish brown and common in rocks in some desert regions.

Often evidence of chemical weathering can be seen as a rind, or covering, surrounding an unweathered core of rock. When cracked in half, boulders found in the field may show weathering rinds and look like stone-colored watermelons without seeds.

Mechanical Weathering. Rocks are also subject to change through the larger physical work of unburial, ice, salt, and vegetation. As overlying sediments are stripped away from large bodies of igneous rock, the pressures of burial that confined them are released, and the rocks often break open. This breakage resulting from pressure release is called jointing, which may occur in straight or curved sheets or layers pulling away from the rock. Other mechanical weathering processes may enlarge the joints. Water may move through them and deposit crystals of salt, which wedge the joints open farther. Or the water may freeze to ice, expanding and pushing the joint walls

jointing

exfoliating granite

Two types of jointing in rocks. Vertical and horizontal joints intersect in a sandstone cliff to form a joint system. Rocks such as these, broken by more than one set of joints, are particularly susceptible to weathering. Uncovered granitic bodies commonly release pressure along curved surfaces, forming sheets known as exfoliating granite.

farther apart. And plant roots may invade the cracks, wedging them open as the plants grow larger.

GLACIAL ACTIVITY

Glaciers form where snow accumulates over many seasons. More snow falls in winter than can melt in warmer months, mostly in the polar regions of the globe and at high, mountainous elevations. Usually the snow deepens gradually, building layers that recrystallize to ice. Recrystallization of snow to ice occurs under the pressure and weight of accumulating snow, as when sediments change through diagenesis and metamorphism to hard rocks. From the accumulation and compaction of snow, a glacier develops, to become a permanent body of ice or recrystallized snow. As the snow and ice pile up, the pull of the earth's gravity becomes stronger on the growing glacier, drawing it outward from its center, down mountains, through valleys, or over gently sloping, open land.

Glaciers can be classified into three groups: valley, piedmont, and continental. Valley glaciers, also called alpine or mountain glaciers, are those that form at the heads of mountain valleys. They move down through old stream valleys, which may be filled with rivers of glacial ice. Valley glaciers may range from a few hundred square yards to many square miles, as short as a few hundred yards or as long as many dozens of miles. Valley glaciers are common in mountains such as the Alps, Himalayas, Rockies, Sierra Nevada, and Cascades.

A piedmont glacier forms when two or more valley glaciers flow from mountain valleys to join on the plains below. The resulting piedmont glacier is a broad, rounded mass of ice. One of the best-known piedmont glaciers is the Malaspina Glacier in Yakutat Bay, Alaska. The product of joined valley glaciers from several mountain valleys on nearby Mount St. Elias, the Malaspina Glacier covers 1,500 square miles (3,800 square kilometers).

A continental glacier, or ice sheet, spreads outward from its center until it covers much of a landmass or continent. Continental glaciers are usually extremely thick, covering both the high and low points of a continent. The world's largest ice sheet, on the continent of Antarctica, is 10,000 feet (3,000 meters) thick in places and covers an area almost twice as large as the United States. Greenland's ice sheet is also quite large—11,000 feet (3,300 meters) thick in some areas and approximately 670,000 square miles (1.7 million square kilometers) in surface area. During the Ice Age, the Pleistocene Epoch, 2 million years ago, continental glaciers occupied much of the northern parts of North America, Europe, and Asia. Sea level dropped more than 330 feet (100 meters) as much of the earth's water was taken up as ice.

As a glacier pushes down over a land surface, it scratches and carves the rock over which it travels. The glacier scrapes over weathered rock and soil, carrying them away, traveling at the rate of a few centimeters to a few meters each day. At the base of the glacier are rocks and sediment that it has picked up along the way. The massive weight of the glacial ice, combined with the

Glacial striations on a rock surface. Erratics, boulders of a rock type different from the underlying bedrock, were stranded when the glacier retreated.

landforms carved by glaciers

Tarns, small lakes of meltwater, fill bowl-like cirques carved out by repeated thawing and freezing of glaciated peaks. Several tarns stepping in succession down a mountain form a glacial staircase. Tarns often fill with sediment, gradually becoming meadows.

tarn

tarn

Cirques are broad, scooped-out amphitheaters. The cirques pictured here are at the top of a glacial staircase.

Horns result from glacial quarrying on several sides of a mountain.

scraping of embedded rocks, leaves behind grooves and scratches in the ground surface over which the glacier passes. The size of the grooves depends on the size of the rocks carried by the ice. Larger rock fragments cause deeper, wider glacial grooves. Smaller rock fragments leave long, parallel scratches called glacial striations. Fine sand and silt polish the underlying rock like sandpaper, giving it a smooth, shiny surface. Glacial features are scraped in parallel rows, in the direction the glacier flowed. Geologists can study such glacial features to reconstruct the past movement of glaciers in ancient times.

Given time, valley glaciers carve out spectacular landforms characteristic of the world's high mountains—cirques, tarns, horns, glacial valleys, and fjords. Distinctive and common, cirques are the bowl-shaped depressions seen near mountain peaks. A cirque is carved out as meltwater from a snowbank just above snow line percolates into the rock below, refreezing, expanding, and dislodging fragments until a hollow is created. Over time and repeated thawing and freezing, the cirque grows. It fills with snow, and because the snow-filled hollow is above snow line, its contents may remain for many seasons. Eventually the cirque may hold an alpine glacier that helps erode and enlarge it. Some cirques hold small deep lakes, known as tarns, at their downhill edges. If cirques sculpt several sides of a mountain peak, they carve out enough rock all around to form a horn, a pointed peak such as that which crowns the Matterhorn in the European Alps.

The deep valleys left behind when valley glaciers retreat have dished, rounded profiles, unlike the V-shaped canyons carved by rivers. These glacial valleys, when near sea level and filled with ocean water, become fjords.

Ice sheets, on the other hand, may completely wipe out the major surface features of a large area. Because of the great depth and size of the ice sheet, mountains, hills, and valleys will be smoothed out. As the ice sheet spreads, it bulldozes all that lies before it. Such glacial erosion during the Pleistocene Epoch created the large expanses of level prairie in the interior United States and Canada.

Glaciers scrape out broad, U-shaped valleys with nearly vertical sides.

Rivers and streams carve V-shaped canyons, developed as flowing water cuts down and material wastes from the canyon sides.

Fjords are glacial valleys filled with water. Their U-shaped profiles are submerged, so only their steep sides rising from the sea are visible.

WIND ACTION

Wind is also an important means of erosion, mainly in desert regions where little vegetation grows to stabilize or hold down soil and rock. Desert regions are those in which the amount of precipitation received in the area is less than its evaporation rate—in other words, more moisture evaporates from the landscape than can be replaced by rainfall. In moister climates, a cover of plants usually protects the soil so that wind is less effective in removing it. In deserts and other barren landscapes, however, many landforms are clearly wind formed, and the land lies stark and bare in places where wind erosion has stripped it clean.

The movement of windblown sediment in part mirrors the movement of stream-carried sediment. Some particles will roll; others will be lifted above the ground surface. A particle's path through the wind depends on both the size of the particle and the speed of the wind. A 10-mile-per-hour (16-kilometer-per-hour) wind will begin rolling a sand-sized particle. Increasing wind speed increases disturbance or turbulence at the ground level, causing the sand particle to travel by jumping, or saltating, a short distance. The process of saltation accounts for most of the sediment movement in sand-covered areas.

As sand and other sediment are moved across a landscape, erosional features are left behind. Rocks are abraded, or scratched, by wind-driven clasts. Any stone left behind that has been abraded and shaped by wind-carried sand is called a ventifact, a word derived from the Latin words *ventus* for "wind," and *factus* meaning "made or done"—hence, made by wind. Ventifacts cover the surfaces of intensely windblown landscapes, like the Victoria Valley in Antarctica, a bare area buffeted by frequent strong winds off the East Antarctic Ice Sheet. Other erosion-caused features include desert pavement, a cobblestonelike covering left on the floor of a desert after the wind winnows sand from among cobbles, and deflation basins, trough-shaped depressions from which sediment has been removed by wind. Deflation basins are common in the Great Plains of North America, from Canada to Texas. The basins are generally less than 1.5 miles (less than 2.4 kilometers) long and 1 yard (almost 1 meter) deep. They fill with lakes in wet years. In the Libyan Desert of western

saltating grains of sand

Fine particles of silt and clay blow above the ground; the heavier sand grains bounce along in a movement called saltation.

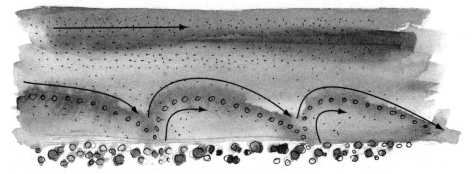

Still larger pebbles blown by the wind may roll along the surface.

features caused by wind erosion

A ventifact, formed and polished by winds in Antarctica.

Desert pavement, a surface of wind-scoured pebbles, remains after the wind carries off smaller particles of silt and sand.

A deflation basin is a trough-shaped depression scoured out by wind. Some depression basins are so big that their structures are difficult to discern from within.

Egypt, an immense deflation basin called the Qattara Depression lies more than 60 miles (100 kilometers) below sea level. In that environment, the winds were strong and persistent and the sediment particularly erodible. Those two factors, erodibility and erosive force, help determine how much material will be lost from a landscape.

TO DO

MOVING WATER

What you will need

large glass jar

sand and pebbles

water

spoon

notebook

You can model the erosive effects of water moving in a stream, using a hand-ful of sand and pebbles and a glass jar.

Cover the bottom of the jar with the sand and pebbles (fish aquarium rock and marbles may be substituted). Add water to fill the jar three-quarters full. Let the sediment settle for a few minutes. Once the sediment has formed a layer at the bottom, stir the water with the spoon. Be careful not to touch the sediment with the spoon—the idea is to let just the water move the sediment. Begin by stirring slowly. What happens? Now stir faster. Remove the spoon and observe. Make notes and drawings in your notebook. As the water slows down, what happens to the sediments? Do the lighter or heavier materials drop out of the current first? What happens to the pebbles? What can you conclude about loose material affected by moving water?

Explanation: When water moves quickly in a streambed or over a surface of loose sediments, the sediments move in a manner similar to those in your jar. The lighter particles are suspended and carried away in the process of stream erosion, which is nothing more than the process you noted in the jar. If the water moves quickly and forcefully, even larger particles are affected. A surface will be changed and rearranged, and the sediments will be redeposited wherever the waning currents drop them.

You can observe the effects of stream erosion in the field, too, as in the next activity.

OBSERVING STREAM LOADS

What you will need

outdoor clothes

equipment for hiking or boating

notebook

Some of life's most pleasurable activities, wandering along streambeds and rafting or canoeing on rivers, are also excellent ways to study stream loads.

Start by strolling along a creek near your home. If you take off your shoes and walk in the water, you can feel the creekbed with your feet. What features can you feel in the creekbottom? Is it composed of bedrock, pebbles, or sand and mud? You may notice that different stretches have different compositions. If so, sketch the shape and length of the creek and note where bottom changes occur.

Does the water appear to carry sediment? Are rocks scattered over the surface of the bed individually or in groups? Where are they with respect to side creeks, pools, the stream current, and the main channel? Create a map of your stream with regard to its current and draw conclusions about how sediments are moved from place to place, thereby undergoing erosion and deposition.

If you are able to float a river by raft or canoe, notice where rapids, pools, and eddies form. Do you see rocks, sediment, and scoured-out places? Where are they in the overall scheme of the river? Are rapids in wide, narrow, or shallow places? Or are they in all three places and more? If so, how do they differ in each place? Look down through the water, and make notes about whether it is free of sediment or full of silt. If you can see any of the river's bed load, sketch it with respect not only to the streambanks but also to side creeks and canyons.

Explanation: If you write and sketch your observations, you will find patterns and connections among them with respect to how sediment is moved into and by a creek or river. Rocks and debris eroding from side creeks and canyons into a main river channel often spread out into or partially block the current, to form the rocky river passages called rapids. The fine suspended load in creek water may be dropped in its slower passages to blanket the creekbottom. Eroded places include the scoured-out basins of rock that form pools, the cut banks on the outside of meanders, and the edges of sandbars that are carried away with shifts in current. What places did you sketch that seem to have been formed by erosion?

SIMULATING WIND AND ICE

What you will need

pieces of dark and light paper

small glass jar

freezerproof container

garden or work gloves

notebook

You can simulate the effects of wind and ice on rock by collecting and testing a few samples.

Gather several rock samples. Make sure you have two samples of each type you collect. Rub together two of the same kind of rock above a piece of paper—if the rocks are light in color, rub them over dark paper; if dark in color, use light paper. Then set the rocks on the paper near the particles that fell. Are the particles the same color as the rocks? Are the rocks scratched where they were rubbed together? Follow the same procedure for each pair of rocks. In your notebook, write your observations, not only about how each set of rocks appeared after rubbing, but how the sets compared. Which rocks created the most particles when rubbed? Which show the most scratches?

Next, fill a small glass jar to the top with water. Close the lid of the jar securely and set it inside the freezerproof container (a bowl or pan tightly covered with foil will work). Leave the jar and container in the freezer overnight. When you remove them later, note the changes that have occurred in the water and glass.

Be sure to wear gloves to protect your hands in case anything has broken in the container overnight.

Explanation: When the wind blows sand against rock, it erodes and abrades much as the rubbing together of your samples did. When water freezes inside rocks, it behaves much as your freezing experiment did. Both erosive agents are powerful forces in changing the earth's surface. Think about where you see such erosion at work in the field, and watch for similar effects among rocks.

TO THINK ABOUT

The Soil Profile. All the soil we see on the ground, commonly called dirt, is made of eroded pieces of rock. Soil scientists call the succession of soil types, from the highly weathered material at the surface to the less weathered material at depth, the soil horizon. Soil develops in two ways: either as pieces of rock eroded in place from underlying bedrock or as pieces transported from other sources.

In the first process, weathering begins at the ground surface and works downward, penetrating into bedrock, sometimes to depths of many meters. In the second process, material weathers before it is transported to its place in the soil profile—say as material carried by water from bedrock in the mountains to accumulate in a valley or on a floodplain. In either case, working from ground surface downward, soil profiles define soil layers in terms of the A, B, C, and D horizons: The A horizon is the top layer, sometimes rich in organic matter; the B horizon, the next layer down, is less fertile but still rich in minerals; the C horizon is a transition zone between soil and unweathered

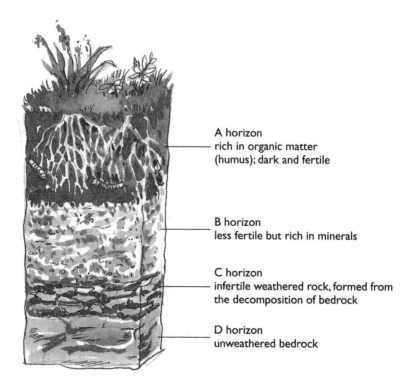

A horizon
rich in organic matter
(humus); dark and fertile

B horizon
less fertile but rich in minerals

C horizon
infertile weathered rock, formed from
the decomposition of bedrock

D horizon
unweathered bedrock

The horizons in a sample soil profile.

bedrock; and the D horizon is unweathered bedrock. You can see the layers of the soil profile in cliffs and roadcuts, and you can expose it in your garden if you dig down far enough (see chapter 4, "To Do).

Lahars. Geologists call mudflows composed of volcanic debris and water lahars, a Javanese word. Lahars, rather than hot lava, were responsible for the terrible destruction wrought by the eruption of Colombia's Nevada del Ruiz on November 13, 1985. Nevada del Ruiz is in the Andes, part of the Pacific Ring of Fire. Volcanism in the Andes is attributed to the subduction of oceanic crust in the Nazca Plate beneath the continental crust of South America (see chapter 2).

The volcanic event was fairly minor, but enough magma rose and erupted to melt about 10 percent of the volcano's sizable ice cap. The meltwater along with the eruption of ash and rock formed a massive lahar of liquid and debris. Citizens living near Ruiz had plenty of warning before the eruption occurred. Earthquakes had been common in the area in late 1984, and minor eruptions became more frequent throughout 1985. Volcanic tremors started on November 10 and continued for three days. By November 12, people noticed a strong sulfur smell, warning of pending eruption. At 3:00 P.M. on November 13, officials in a nearby town recommended evacuation of the town of Armero, 30 miles (50 kilometers) down a narrow river canyon from Ruiz. The Armero radio station, however, urged citizens to stay calm. Most did so and lay asleep in their beds at 11:15 P.M., when the mudflow hit the village. The mudflows had traveled down the canyon of the Lagunilla River, 130 feet (40 meters) deep and traveling 25 miles (40 kilometers) an hour. The mud buried the town. Of the population of twenty-three thousand, only about three thousand people escaped alive.

The extreme loss of life could have been avoided, had people followed precautions. How can such future disasters be avoided, not only in river canyons in the Andes, but in other volcanic landscapes around the world as well? Engineers in Japan have constructed check dams along mudflow routes to slow lahars headed for populous areas. What other precautions could be taken?

TO READ

Carroll, Dorothy. *Rock Weathering*. New York: Plenum Press, 1970. A classic reference on the erosion of rock to soil.

Dixon, Dougal. *The Practical Geologist*. New York: Simon and Schuster, 1992. This book contains intelligent activities, excellent illustrations, and a clear, well-written chapter on erosion.

Hunt, C. B. *The Geology of Soils*. San Francisco: W. H. Freeman and Company, 1972. A close look at the geologic aspects of soils and the elements they contain.

Rudner, Ruth. *Forgotten Pleasures: A Guide for the Seasonal Adventurer.* New York: Penguin Books, 1978. Wonderful wanderings through various outdoor environments lead the amateur scientist into creekbeds and rivers, among other places.

Shelton, John S. *Geology Illustrated*. San Francisco: W. H. Freeman, 1966. This book is a must. Landforms photographed from the air and interpreted geologically include many in erosional landscapes.

TO WATCH

Backbone of the Earth: The Story of Tibet. People's Republic of China, 1978. Contains footage of landslides and rock and snow avalanches in the Himalayas. Available through the United States Geological Survey.

Debris Flow Dynamics. Open-File Report 84-606. United States Geological Survey, 1984. Shows Japanese and Chinese footage of landslides. Contains instructive terms and vocabulary regarding mass wasting.

Erosion: Earth Is Change. Children's Television Workshop, 1991. Examines earth changes from hurricanes, earthquakes, volcanoes, and wind and water erosion. Includes a helicopter view of erosive changes in the Grand Canyon.

Hubbard Glacier—Russell Fjord. United States Geological Survey, 1986. Mountains, glaciers, and fjords in Alaska.

Landslide: The 1979 Abbotsford Disaster. University of Otago, 1984. A New Zealand landslide caused by a municipal water line leak and quarrying at the toe of a hill. Available through the United States Geological Survey.

CHAPTER 7

Water:
What Goes Up

In the years since water was created during the formation of our planet, earth's water supply has neither grown nor shrunk. The water of ancient oceans that held the first primitive creatures is still being moved through the hydrologic cycle, a great system of change for all the water on earth. The hydrologic cycle has no beginning or end. It is a ring of time and travel, from ocean up to sky, down to earth, and back to ocean. To make its way through the cycle, water must change phases from liquid to gas, gas to solid, solid to liquid. Water rises as gas, or vapor, from the ocean to the sky; forms into great clouds of ice and water; falls back to earth as rain, snow, hail, and other types of precipitation; and flows over and under the ground, eventually back to the sea.

Geologists must understand water and its cycle for several reasons. Water flowing over the ground deposits sand, clay, and gravel, material for sedimentary rocks. Water is also a powerful agent of erosion, shaping and sculpting

Dinosaurs swam in the same water that we drink today—water that has circulated through the hydrologic cycle for millions of years.

the three phases of the substance water

Gaseous water (steam or vapor) is made when liquid water boils at 212 degrees Fahrenheit (100 degrees C).

Water pours from the tap as a liquid.

At 32 degrees F (0 degrees C) and below, water freezes, turning into solid ice.

DISCOVER NATURE IN THE ROCKS

both soft and hard rock. And some water, groundwater, flows underground, through soil and porous rock.

Water is the only substance on earth that exists naturally in all three possible phases a substance can take: solid, liquid, and gas. More often, a compound takes only two forms; for example, gold is found most often as a solid, but at extremely high temperatures (above 1,948 degrees F or 1,063 degrees C) can be melted and poured as a liquid. On the surface of the earth, however, gold is not found as a gas. Its boiling point temperature is simply too high (5,576 degrees F or 3,077 degrees C), impossible for nature to achieve except far below the earth's crust. Water, however, occurs as a gas nearly everywhere, as water vapor in the air.

Water has many other unusual properties. As a liquid, it can dissolve many hard substances. It has much higher boiling and freezing points than substances with similar molecular structures, such as hydrogen selenide and hydrogen sulfide, two toxic, colorless gases. And upon freezing, whereas other liquids shrink and become more dense, water expands and grows less dense. If it did not, ice would not float on water, and rather than building as a thin skin on top, protecting deeper water from freezing, it would basically freeze from the bottom up. No life could be found in such frozen, solid bodies of water.

THE WATER MOLECULE

As we have seen, any substance is made of molecules. The water molecule consists of one atom of the element hydrogen and two of oxygen, brought

If water did not become less dense upon freezing, ice would sink rather than float.
Iceberg-dwelling polar bears, deprived of their ice islands, would have to find other homes.

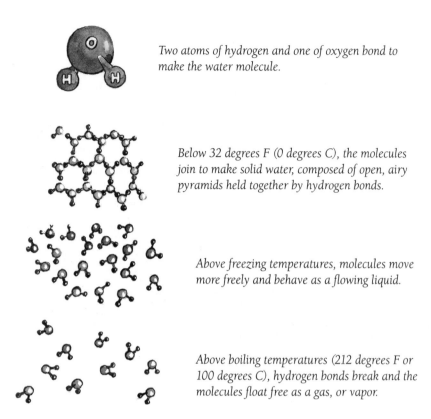

Two atoms of hydrogen and one of oxygen bond to make the water molecule.

Below 32 degrees F (0 degrees C), the molecules join to make solid water, composed of open, airy pyramids held together by hydrogen bonds.

Above freezing temperatures, molecules move more freely and behave as a flowing liquid.

Above boiling temperatures (212 degrees F or 100 degrees C), hydrogen bonds break and the molecules float free as a gas, or vapor.

together in a strong covalent bond, forged by atoms sharing electrons. The atoms are more stable when joined, so they are unlikely to break apart. In water, the two elements are drawn together so strongly that a tremendous amount of energy, such as heat, must be used to divide them.

Water's covalent bond is so strong that the molecule easily wedges between atoms of other substances, breaking their weaker bonds. If water and table salt are stirred together, for example, the water molecules break the weaker bonds in the salt. The salt crystals separate, or dissolve, into their two elements, sodium and chloride. Water is so good at dissolving other compounds that it is rarely found in its pure state, unmixed with other atoms.

Water also willingly joins with the molecules of some solids. It binds with glass, clay, or soil, solids containing oxygen atoms that attract water's hydrogen atoms (an attraction called a hydrogen bond). A film of water coating a drinking glass is an example of water molecules binding with solids. Also because of its ability to attach to other substances, water climbs easily through small vessels, such as test tubes or plant veins, even against the force of gravity. Upward

Water travels from the ground through plants by means of capillary action.

The roots, stems, and leaf veins are channels through which water molecules are drawn, to be transpired as vapor into the air from the surfaces of leaves.

Sequoiadendron giganteum, standing 300 feet (91 meters) tall, draws 300 gallons (1,136 liters) of water each day from the ground. That rate of capillary action yields 2,500 pounds (1,134 kilograms) of water brought into the air daily, as if by a geyser.

movement by capillary action is made possible by water linking with the molecules of the vessel walls and working its way progressively higher.

Whether water assumes its solid, liquid, or gaseous phase depends on its temperature. When water is cooled to below 32 degrees F (0 degrees C), its molecules arrange into crystal structures, spacious pyramid shapes joined together by hydrogen bonds. These open structures account for water's greater size as it freezes, taking up more room as it crystallizes. At higher temperatures, the molecules become more active. Above the freezing point, the bonds break and shift, and the molecules move around more freely, so much so that water becomes a flowing liquid. Above the boiling point (212 degrees F or 100 degrees C), water molecules break their bonds and float free, turning to gas, or vapor.

SURFACE WATER

Once water precipitates, it can become surface water, with a great ability to quickly change a landscape. As runoff, it soaks the soil and flattens plants. It can cause flooding, moving sediment from areas that are usually not wet and so are loose and easily washed away. In moist areas with many plants, soil is held in place by plant roots. Soil and plants help soak up the runoff, so flood waters may rise and fall more slowly. But in desert areas with little vegetation and exposed soils, runoff is swift in flash floods after hard rains from thunderstorms. Dry washes erode, gullies are carved, and the landscape changes rapidly.

Lakes, rivers, and streams contain surface water that is on its way back to the ocean. These bodies of water are the most visible movers and containers of runoff. Most runoff, however, soaks underground, filtering through tiny air spaces in soil and rock to become groundwater, where 97 percent of the world's fresh water lies.

GROUNDWATER

Early scientists believed that groundwater flowed in huge rivers and channels beneath the earth. The Greek philosopher Plato, who lived and taught around 400 B.C., believed that the ocean flowed underground into a big river known as the River Styx. As it flowed, the salt water in the underground river was thought to be made fresh before returning to the surface.

Today we know that groundwater does flow underground, but not in large rivers or into great sucking canyons beneath the ocean; rather, it flows through spaces between grains of sand and gravel in soil and rock. The speed

the hydrologic cycle

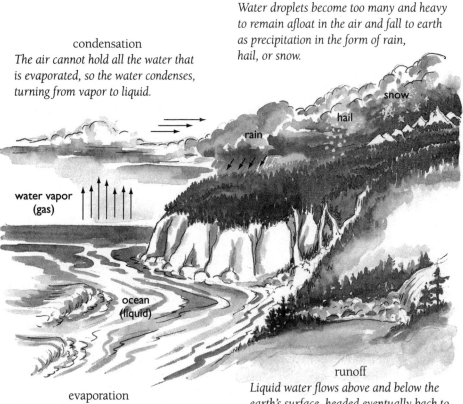

precipitation
Water droplets become too many and heavy to remain afloat in the air and fall to earth as precipitation in the form of rain, hail, or snow.

condensation
The air cannot hold all the water that is evaporated, so the water condenses, turning from vapor to liquid.

snow

hail

rain

water vapor (gas)

ocean (liquid)

evaporation
The sun warms the water's surface, causing molecular bonds to break and liquid to turn to vapor.

runoff
Liquid water flows above and below the earth's surface, headed eventually back to the ocean to begin the cycle again.

of water movement is determined by the size of spaces between grains in soil and rock. If the spaces are small, water will flow very slowly. If the spaces are larger, water will flow more quickly. Rock that allows the passage of water is called permeable rock. Groundwater may flow through permeable rock as quickly as 30 feet (10 meters) per day.

Once surface water seeps through soil and rock, it travels downward to the zone of saturation, a zone of permeable rock in which all the air spaces are saturated, or filled, with groundwater. The top of the zone of saturation is called the water table, which can be near the ground surface or far below.

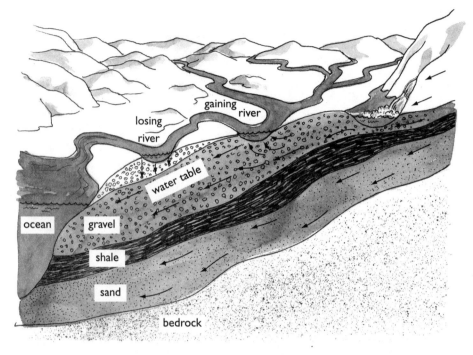

This picture shows three aspects of underground water travel: to rivers that gain water from or lose water to the water table because of differences in water pressure, through rock that allows the flow of water, and to the ocean.

Water passes quickly through the large spaces between the grains of gravel.

Shale allows minimal water movement because the pores in which water is stored are not connected.

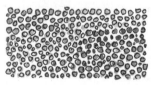

Sand allows the passage of water, but the rate of water movement is slower because the pores are smaller.

Groundwater travels through gravel, sand, and shale at different rates depending on the size of spaces, or pores, in the rock and how connected they are.

Where the water table is high, it can be seen at the surface as lakes and streams. Where the water table crosses cracks and cliffs in the ground, it flows out as springs.

Water seeps downward underground until it reaches beds of rocks that it cannot penetrate. This impermeable rock acts as a barrier that forces the water to flow horizontally because it cannot go farther down. Then the water flows in the direction that it is being pulled most strongly—toward a spring, toward a well pumping water back to the surface for drinking water, or toward the bed of a river that is flowing back to the sea.

Groundwater, like all water, is part of the hydrologic cycle moving water from the sea to land to sea again. Although it might be moving slowly, groundwater is still making its way through the rocks and back to the ocean, there to begin the great process again: evaporation, condensation, precipitation, runoff.

TO DO

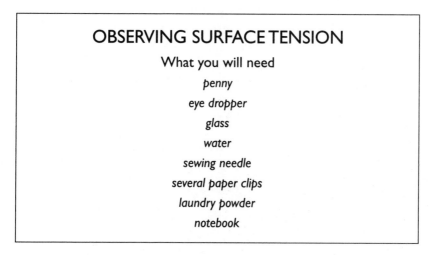

OBSERVING SURFACE TENSION

What you will need

penny

eye dropper

glass

water

sewing needle

several paper clips

laundry powder

notebook

The surface of water—be it in a glass, lake, or river—is covered by a tough film or skin. You can watch it in action in a few easy experiments.

Start by filling the glass to the brim with water. It should be full to the top but not overflowing. One by one, add the paper clips gently to the glass of water. Try not to splash and upset the surface. Observe the water surface. Does it stay level? When does the water spill over? Note the results in your notebook.

Now set a penny on a table or desk. Guess how many water droplets will fit on the top of the coin before they spill over. Write your estimate in your notebook. Using the eyedropper, transfer water droplets from the glass to the penny. Observe what happens. Do you see evidence of a skin forming on the water? Write and sketch the results in your notebook.

Next, now that the water level in the glass is somewhat below the rim, carefully float the needle on the surface of the water. Sketch a picture of the floating needle in your notebook. Remember that the needle is made of steel, which weighs more than an equal volume of water. Add a pinch of laundry powder to the glass and watch what happens.

Explanation: The attractive force between water molecules is called cohesion. Because of cohesion, water forms into droplets with distinctive shapes. Also because of cohesion, water molecules cling together in a tough film of skin on water surfaces, a property known as surface tension. We see evidence of surface tension everywhere: in a kitchen sink where a water droplet hangs from the tap without breaking, at the feet of insects that float on lakes without sinking, and at the edges of droplets that gather on leaves and rocks. The laundry powder breaks up the surface tension by disturbing the cohesion of the water molecules.

Surface tension is an important property in terms of rock and soil erosion. Because a tough surface skin surrounds each raindrop that falls, drops can hit rocks with enough force to gradually break them down and over time wash them away.

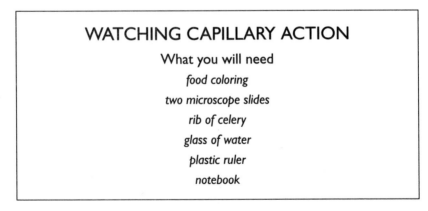

WATCHING CAPILLARY ACTION

What you will need

food coloring

two microscope slides

rib of celery

glass of water

plastic ruler

notebook

Capillary action is easily demonstrated using food coloring and celery stalks.

Mix a few drops of food coloring into the water in the glass. Squeeze the two microscope slides together. Dip just one corner of the slides into the colored water. What happens? How quickly does it happen? Next, trim the bottom off a rib of celery and put it bottom down in the glass of water. Set your experiment aside for a few days. Take notes every day, using your ruler to measure changes in the celery. Record dates and times along with your observations.

Explanation: Besides the property of cohesion (attraction of its molecules for each other), water has the property of adhesion (attraction of its molecules for those of other substances). In the first part of this experiment, water molecules are attracted to the molecules in glass, so they reach and climb along the slides to find more glass molecules. The water molecules pull more water molecules in a chain behind them. This pulling-up action, called capillary action, uses both the properties of cohesion and adhesion. The action continues until the column is too long and heavy to overcome gravity and the chain stops its upward movement. Water will rise higher in a narrow tube than a wide one because the hydrogen atoms at the edge of the water must lift fewer molecules behind it to make progress up the tube.

Water's capillary action gives it the ability to flow through small spaces, like the veins in a stalk of celery and the connected pores in soil and rock.

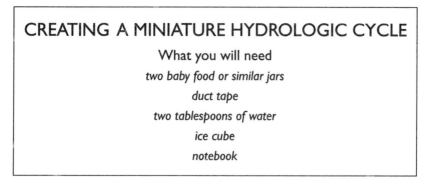

CREATING A MINIATURE HYDROLOGIC CYCLE

What you will need
two baby food or similar jars

duct tape

two tablespoons of water

ice cube

notebook

You can build your own enclosed hydrologic cycle and watch the process of change.

Place the water and ice cube in one jar. Tape the jars together, mouth to mouth, and stand them in a sunny location. Observe what happens to the ice cube and the level of the water. Sketch and note the results. Check the jars each day for a week, noting dates and times along with any observations of what happens inside the jars.

Explanation: The cycle is solar powered, as your miniature system shows. No part of the cycle—not ice, rain, surface water, or groundwater—would change without the energy of the sun. Its heat is a great pumping force, driving the lifeblood of the entire planet. No matter where water is in the cycle, whether making its way through soil and rock back to the ocean or whether bound up in ice, the sun's heat assures that water enters the cycle again.

STORING HEAT

What you will need

two coffee cans

water

soil

kitchen oven

meat thermometer

notebook

Water stores heat effectively, as can be easily demonstrated.

Preheat your oven to a low temperature, about 150 degrees. If you cannot use an oven, sunlight will work as a warming agent. Fill one can with soil and the other with water. Set them in the preheated oven or sunlight for a few hours. Remove them and measure their temperatures with the thermometer. As they cool, check their changing temperatures with the thermometer. Note the results in your notebook. Which cools down faster, the soil or the water?

Explanation: Water can absorb a lot of heat without changing in temperature. If you've ever burned your hand on the handle of a pot of water set to boil on the stove and noticed that the water inside was still cool, you know the metal of the pot heated up faster than the water, requiring much less energy to raise its temperature one degree.

The opposite process is true for water as well. To take its heat away—that is, to cool it down—takes more energy than many substances require. So the heat is stored in the water for some time while it slowly gives off energy.

Similarly, the heat stored in seawater can warm air traveling inland, often affecting nearby land with warmer airflows. Large lakes can store heat, too.

FLOATING ICE

What you will need

two large ice cubes

glass

notebook

Water in its frozen phase is less dense than liquid water. You can watch this property at work in this experiment.

Place the ice cubes in the glass, and fill it to the top with water, as full as possible without its overflowing. The ice should extend above the water surface and stick up beyond the top of the glass. Sketch a picture. Imagine the ice cubes as tiny icebergs in a small sea. How much of the ice floats? How much is visible above the surface?

Observe what happens as the ice melts. The water and the ice cubes did not fit inside the glass, so one would expect the water to overflow the glass as it all becomes liquid. Does it happen? Sketch your results.

Explanation: In its frozen state, water is about 10 percent larger in volume than in its liquid state. It floats in liquid water because it is lighter. The action of water enlarging upon freezing is an important agent of erosion in rock during freeze-thaw cycles. A good visual sense of floating ice is also helpful when studying the principle of isostasy with respect to continental and oceanic crust, as discussed in the next chapter.

TO THINK ABOUT

Drinking Water. Water flows underground through permeable water-bearing layers of rock known as aquifers. Water in aquifers can easily flow to wells and springs. In the United States, aquifers are found under more than half the land surface. Many people count on the water in aquifers for drinking water: Forty-eight thousand community water systems and 12 million individual water wells supply drinking water across the country. Many of the nation's largest cities rely on groundwater from aquifers for drinking water.

Groundwater in aquifers is very high in quality, protected from most pollution by overlying rock and soil. Groundwater is therefore a great natural resource. On the other hand, the water table drops in times of drought, and some wells dry up. In some fast-growing cities especially, more groundwater is being pumped from aquifers than can be replaced through the slow flow of groundwater, and water tables are falling so quickly that the overlying ground surface is dropping as well. Las Vegas, Nevada, for example, has grown so fast recently that increased groundwater use has caused the surrounding valley floor to sink, in some places as much as 5 feet (1.5 meters).

Contamination of Groundwater. Although groundwater is more protected from polluting sources than surface water, we now know that groundwater can be polluted. One of the greatest threats to groundwater quality is old trash dumps, or landfills. We once believed that anything could be thrown unenclosed into landfills: car oil, cans of paint, spray cans, dead animals, dirty diapers. Now we know that contaminants from such refuse do not just stay where they are dumped; instead, they seep down through the soil to the groundwater. As a result, various polluting chemicals have reached aquifers, especially near heavily populated areas.

Once groundwater has become impure, it is hard to clean it up because contaminants often adhere to the soil. Hydrogeologists, geologists who study groundwater and its associated rock, drill borings and install monitoring wells to sample and test groundwater for chemicals. Although cleanup of a contaminated aquifer can be costly, certain chemicals cause severe health problems in humans and animals and must be extracted. Contaminants such as those found in old landfills must be removed and others prevented from entering groundwater.

Waiting It Out. When rainwater seeps in and becomes groundwater, it may not return to the active hydrologic cycle for many, sometimes even thousands, of years. No water is ever permanently out of the cycle, however; even rain that has fallen many thousands of years ago and is trapped miles beneath the earth's surface eventually finds its way back up. Today, a molecule of water spends an average of nine days in the atmosphere, two weeks in rivers, ten years in large lakes, tens to hundreds of years in groundwater, three thousand years in the oceans, and ten thousand years in shallow groundwater. A molecule of water can also stop out of the cycle for ten thousand years in a polar ice cap. About 2 percent of the earth's water is stored in glaciers, huge moving sheets of ice.

One million years ago, during a colder time known as an ice age, more of the earth's water was stored in ice. The glaciers spread over about half of North America, grinding down mountains and gouging out huge lake basins. As more of the earth's water became taken up in ice, the sea levels dropped. Continents grew in size. Shallow land beneath the English Channel was exposed, linking England and Europe. Asia and Alaska were joined by a land bridge. Scientists believe that such freezing had happened before, during at least two earlier ice ages.

Eventually the planet warmed again and many glaciers melted, putting more liquid water back in circulation. But no one knows for sure if the planet is still warming in a trend that will cause serious global changes or if we will see another ice age.

TO READ

Arnov, Boris. *Water: Experiments to Understand It.* New York: Lothrop, Lee & Shepard Books, 1980. Experiments and explanations of many aspects of water's behavior.

Leopold, Luna, Kenneth S. Davis, and the editors of Time-Life Books. *Water.* Alexandria, VA: Time-Life Books, 1980. An excellent book about the nature of water in all its phases and uses.

National Geographic Society. *Water: The Power, Promise, and Turmoil of North America's Fresh Water.* Washington, DC: National Geographic Society, 1993. This special edition takes readers across North America to see how water is used and abused.

Reisner, Marc. *Cadillac Desert: The American West and Its Disappearing Water.* New York: Viking Penguin, 1987. A must-read account of Western groundwater and surface water resources.

TO WATCH

Down the Drain. Children's Television Workshop, 1991. An excellent and fun video about the water cycle.

Eureka! TVOntario, 1981. A series of animated five-minute programs about the behavior of matter, including water, in motion.

Water Cycle: Go With the Flow. Children's Television Workshop, 1991. Experiments show how water is cleaned during its journey through the hydrologic cycle.

CHAPTER 8

Continents: Pieces of the Puzzle

Today scientists more or less agree that the surface of the earth consists of numerous crustal plates embedded in the underlying semimolten layer of upper mantle. Most scientists also agree that these plates are on the move and have been since they began forming about 4 billion years ago. This agreement regarding plate and continental movement, however, is fairly recent. Before the phrase "plate tectonics" was added to geologists' vocabulary beginning around 1968, debate raged on the creation and past configuration of continents on the earth. The story of how scientists came to accept continental movement as a plausible geologic theory is one of the most fascinating tales in the history of science—and a great lesson in independent scientific thinking.

Theories of continental movement date back as far as 1858, when writer Antonio Snider-Pelligrini, attempting to explain why fossils of identical animal species were found on widely separate continents, suggested that all the world's continents had once been joined in a single mass. Today very different species of animals and plants inhabit different continents; no one expected fossil animals and plants to be the same across oceans. Snider-Pelligrini observed that the matching fossils could be explained by reassembling the continents like puzzle pieces. He speculated that Africa and South America had once been joined along their matching coastlines and subsequently split apart, after certain species had developed and spread through the land. He was thus the first person known to publish speculation on large movements by continents over the surface of the earth. He also proposed that Noah's flood was responsible for breaking up the original continental mass, an unpopular notion that brought disrepute to even the meritorious aspects of his theories.

In 1885, Austrian geologist Edward Suess theorized that the continents of the Southern Hemisphere were once united as a greater land mass that he called Gondwanaland. Continents of the Northern Hemisphere were joined into a larger whole called Laurasia. Suess came to these conclusions on the basis of fossil evidence. Fossil remains of *Mesosaurus*, a reptile that lived 270 million years ago, were excavated in Brazil and South Africa. Fossils of the

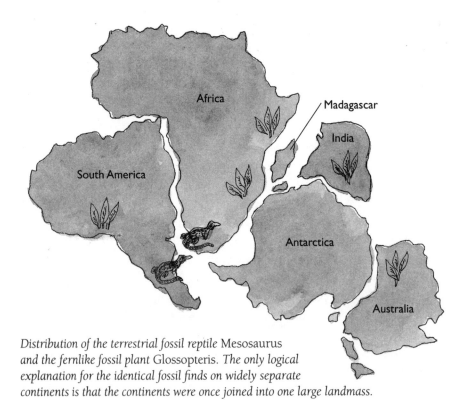

Distribution of the terrestrial fossil reptile Mesosaurus *and the fernlike fossil plant* Glossopteris. *The only logical explanation for the identical fossil finds on widely separate continents is that the continents were once joined into one large landmass.*

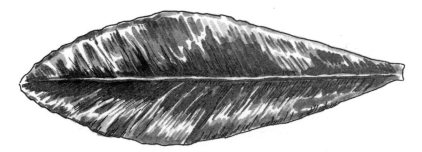

Fossil remains of the primitive fern Glossopteris *have been found in South America, Africa, Madagascar, and Australia.*

Glossopteris fern showed up in both India and Australia. Popular theory in Suess's time held, however, that land bridges had linked the larger masses and subsequently sunk into the ocean as the earth cooled and contracted. Suess's belief that the continents fit snugly together was supported by one major factor—the search for evidence of sunken land bridges on the sea floor was turning up nothing.

In 1908, American geologist Frank Taylor again raised the suggestion that, rather than land bridges sinking to allow continental separation, the continents must be moving horizontally. He explained that great mountain ranges could result from slow continental collisions and even indicated a known line of undersea mountains between South America and Africa as the zone of separation or rifting of continents. Taylor named the mountains the Mid-Atlantic Ridge. Although Taylor was on the right track and had gathered good evidence, his theories were ignored or disputed by his contemporaries, who believed that the positions of continents had remained static through time.

Then, in 1912, German meteorologist Alfred Wegener burst onto the geologic scene with his well-considered views on "The Formation of the Major Features of the Earth's Crust (Continents and Oceans)." A respected scientist but an outsider to the geologic community, Wegener observed that rock, fossil, and climatological evidence suggested that the continents had once been part of a single ancestral landmass. He named the mother continent Pangaea, meaning "all earth." Although popular scientific thought still championed the notion of sunken land bridges, Wegener suggested, as Taylor had, that the continents had drifted apart and continue to drift. Although his theory was ridiculed in his lifetime, he staunchly adhered to it. He suffered endless hostile blasts to his views; fortunately, his successes in other areas, such as meteorology, preserved his reputation. Upon his death in 1930 on a scientific

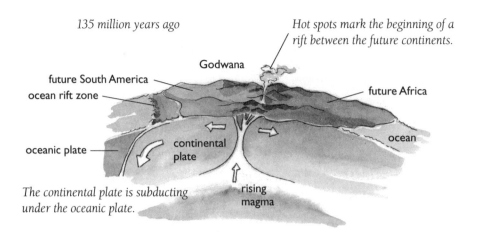

135 million years ago *Hot spots mark the beginning of a rift between the future continents.*

Godwana

future South America
ocean rift zone

future Africa

oceanic plate

continental plate

ocean

The continental plate is subducting under the oceanic plate.

rising magma

A rift valley opens as magma continues to well up, weakening and fracturing the earth's crust. The spreading crust slides and sinks, forming the central rift valley. Other sections of crust are uplifted into mountain ranges.

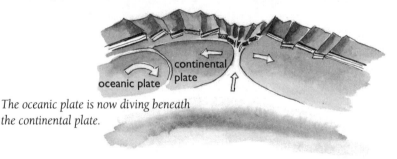

oceanic plate

continental plate

The oceanic plate is now diving beneath the continental plate.

Water from the opening Atlantic Ocean floods in to fill the gap between the continents. Continuing ocean floor spreading widens the rift about 2 inches (5 centimeters) per year.

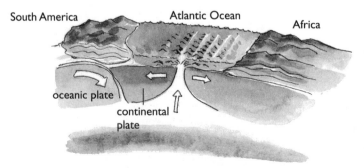

South America

Atlantic Ocean

Africa

oceanic plate

continental plate

Geologist Frank Taylor suggested that the great chain of undersea mountains between South America and Africa was the location of the separation of continents. This drawing shows our current understanding of how the two continents rifted apart.

expedition to Greenland, written tributes largely passed over his theories on continental drift, possibly considered a strange blip in an otherwise successful career. Later, however, his contributions to geology posthumously immortalized him—he became known as the father of the theory of continental drift.

EVIDENCE FOR CONTINENTAL DRIFT

Wegener stuck to his theory in the face of much antagonism from other scientists in part because a growing body of evidence disproved the existence of ancient land bridges between continents. Continental crust was shown to be

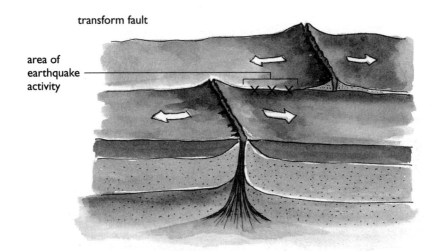

One of Wegener's missing pieces of evidence was a convincing mechanism driving the continents over the globe. As recently as 1959, Canadian geophysicist J. Tuzo Wilson noted the missing mechanism, saying continental drift was a concept "without a cause or physical theory." But, in 1965, Wilson's own interpretation of transform faulting along midocean ridges became one of the most convincing pieces of evidence for continental drift. Transform faults, as shown in this drawing, are offset segments along the length of midocean ridge lines. The fractures between the segments run perpendicular to the main ridge and extend for hundreds of miles (kilometers) on either side of it. For many years, scientists believed the many miles (kilometers) of fractures to be extensive lateral faults and the segments to be pieces of crust moved along those faults. Wilson noticed, however, that earthquakes did not occur everywhere along the fractures, as they would if great blocks of crust were moving past each other. Rather, he noted earthquake activity (associated with opposite motion) only along the short sections of opposite-moving crust between the offset ridges. He therefore concluded that when new crust moved beyond the offset ridge to spread in tandem with crust beside it, earthquake activity was no longer generated. Transform faults, then, are unique among faults: They are unchanging features that resulted from weaknesses when the continents first split apart. Their existence, wrote Wilson in 1965, "would go far towards establishing the reality of continental drift."

much less dense than oceanic crust, making the sinking of continents into the ocean floor impossible. Lighter crustal rocks float in the denser mantle, as icebergs are carried in ocean water. Wegener reasoned that just as icebergs do not sink but break up and float apart, continents have done the same.

Wegener also pointed to the fact that mountains do not form uniformly over the globe, as they would if the popular global cooling and shrinking theory held true. Instead, mountains occur in long, sinuous chains found most often at the edges of continents. Wegener believed the mountain belts resulted when wandering continents encountered others, experiencing increasing resistance and crustal folding. But he failed to suggest a convincing mechanism for continental drift, recognizing that that part of the mystery had yet to be discovered. Over many years, various researchers throughout the world helped unravel the mystery by following diverse lines of evidence such as geochronology, paleoclimatology, and paleomagnetics.

Geochronology. A strong supporter of the continental drift theory was South African geologist Alexander Du Toit, who was familiar with the rocks of his own continent as well as those of South America. In the 1920s, he found the same plant and animal fossils in the same sequence of similar rock layers on both sides of the Atlantic. Scientists of that time were well aware that a strip of only a few miles of water would prevent the spread of a diverse and well-ordered regime of biota. Du Toit noted that the geochronology—the sequence of rocks through time—was largely the same in both the Cape Mountains in South Africa and the Sierra Mountains in Argentina. Scientists since Du Toit have made similar matches among the mountains in eastern Canada, Scotland, and Norway. Strata not only are the same type and age but were deposited in exactly the same order across continents.

Glacial deposits in Africa, South America, Australia, Asia, and Antarctica suggest that all five continents lay under an ice sheet around 270 million years ago, in late Paleozoic time. Observations of glacial striations and till in the deposits suggest that if the continents lay in their present configuration during the Paleozoic Era, movement of the ice sheet would have been toward both poles and away from the equator. Also, the ice sheet would have covered equatorial continents, presenting a climatological impossibility: Because of the earth's orientation to the sun, such massive glaciation is possible at the geographic poles, which receive little radiation, but not at the equator, which receives much. Reassembling the continents in a single southern landmass provides an easier explanation for both phenomena: Ice movement radiated from the glacial center, as it does today in continental glaciers, and the ice sheet covered a single ancestral continent in the region of the South Pole.

Paleoclimatology. By studying glacial evidence on equatorial continents and realizing that the earth's climatic zones had probably not changed drastically with respect to the poles, scientists began to believe that the continents had indeed wandered. Other climatological clues to former continental positions were the discovery of coral reefs (indicators of warm, shallow seas) and coal deposits (indicators of swampy environments) in ancient rock sequences sampled near the North Pole. Rock sequences in some arctic regions also contain salt deposits, indicating past desert climates on lands now icebound throughout the year.

Paleomagnetics. The earth has its own magnetic field, attributable in part to the dynamo, or generator, effect of planetary rotation, with magnetic poles near the South and North Poles. Paleomagnetics, the study of changes in the earth's ancient magnetic fields, offered one of the strongest lines of evidence supporting continental drift. The earth's magnetic field reverses occasionally. Reversals occur anywhere from every sixteen-hundred to twenty-one thousand years. Iron-rich minerals crystallize with their iron molecules aligned parallel to the earth's magnetic field at the time, recording paleomagnetic data directly in rocks as they form. Sensitive magnetic recording instruments called magnetometers read these data and evaluate the corresponding positions of the magnetic poles.

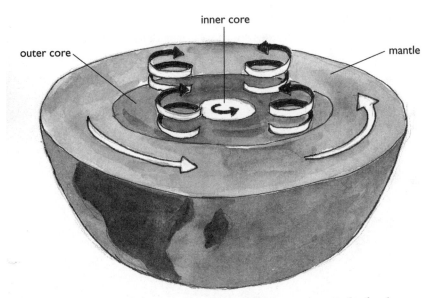

The rotation of the earth and convection of heat combine to create spirals of molten material in the core. Much as electric current flowing through copper coils creates a magnetic field around the wire, the spiraling of the earth generates its magnetic field.

In the 1960s, magnetometers carried back and forth across the Atlantic Ocean revealed strips of ocean floor crust lying parallel to the midocean ridges. These strips were distinguished by their alternating alignment of iron-rich minerals: strips of crust with north-aligned minerals alternated with strips of crust with south-aligned minerals. These alternating alignments resulted when basalt rising along the Mid-Atlantic Ridge cooled and recorded the earth's magnetic field, moving away from the ridge as new basalt came to the surface. When the poles reversed, the newest basalt recorded the reversed magnetic field, with the North Pole at the modern-day South Pole. Thus the magnetic stripes on the ocean floor provided good evidence for midocean spreading.

Magnetometers also measure the inclination of the angle of the magnetic field from horizontal. In the 1950s, magnetometer studies of ancient rocks in England indicated that the iron minerals were aligned to the north at an angle of 30 degrees from horizontal (30 degrees north inclination). Today, the same location in England indicates 65 degrees north inclination. Inclination is 90 degrees north at the North Pole, 0 degrees at the equator, and 90 degrees south at the South Pole. Thus the only logical conclusion was that England must have been farther south when the rocks crystallized at 30 degrees north inclination.

Another interesting piece of evidence is that magnetometers set up in India have recorded an inclination of 64 degrees south for rocks dated 150 million years old and 26 degrees south for rocks dated 50 million years old. Much younger rocks, dated 25 million years old, registered 17 degrees north

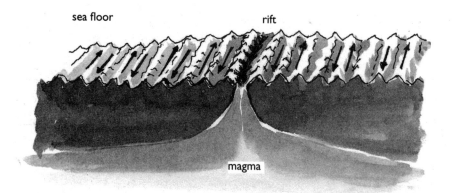

Ancient reversals between the earth's magnetic poles were recorded in iron-rich minerals in oceanic crust, forming alternating strips of normal and reversal-polarity crust on both sides of ocean ridges.

polar wandering

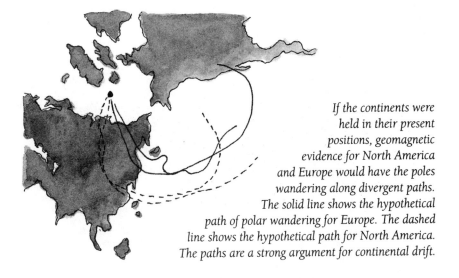

If the continents were held in their present positions, geomagnetic evidence for North America and Europe would have the poles wandering along divergent paths. The solid line shows the hypothetical path of polar wandering for Europe. The dashed line shows the hypothetical path for North America. The paths are a strong argument for continental drift.

inclination. Clearly India had once been in the Southern Hemisphere, crossing the equator to its present position as part of Asia between 50 and 25 million years ago.

Opponents of the concept of continental drift tried to explain away these strong pieces of paleomagnetic evidence by suggesting that the magnetic poles themselves had wandered substantially, and therefore that the rocks in England and India had recorded varying magnetic data without moving from their present positions. If such were true, the North Pole would have wandered 13,000 miles (nearly 21,000 kilometers) in the last billion years, scribing a curvilinear path from western North America, across the Pacific Ocean and northern Asia, to rest finally in the Arctic Ocean. Magnetometer readings in North America and Eurasia showed polar wandering traveling in opposite directions for each continent. When scientists hypothetically joined the two continents, the curved paths overlapped, providing a strong piece of evidence for an ancestral landmass.

HISTORIC PLATE MOVEMENTS

Today scientists believe that at least one ancestral landmass predated Wegener's Pangaea. In the 1960s, geologists working in the Canadian Appalachian Mountains noted the presence of ophiolites, masses of igneous rock, like basalt, with a special composition and structure suggesting that they were

the opening, closing, and reopening of the Atlantic Ocean

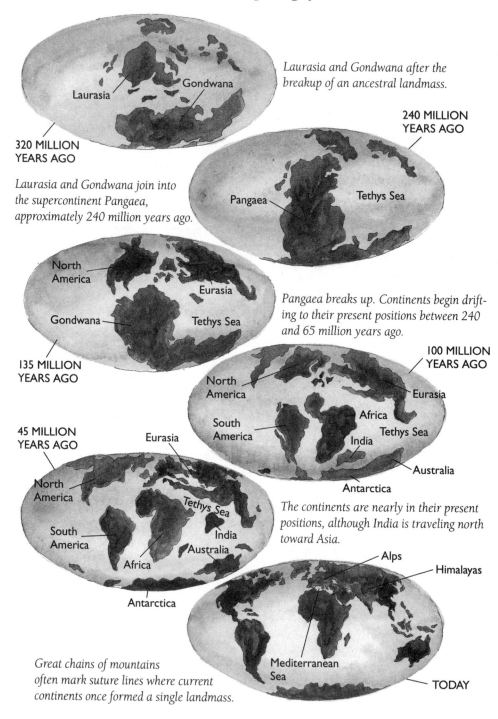

Laurasia and Gondwana after the breakup of an ancestral landmass.

240 MILLION YEARS AGO

320 MILLION YEARS AGO

Laurasia and Gondwana join into the supercontinent Pangaea, approximately 240 million years ago.

Pangaea breaks up. Continents begin drifting to their present positions between 240 and 65 million years ago.

135 MILLION YEARS AGO

100 MILLION YEARS AGO

45 MILLION YEARS AGO

The continents are nearly in their present positions, although India is traveling north toward Asia.

Great chains of mountains often mark suture lines where current continents once formed a single landmass.

TODAY

once pieces of oceanic crust pushed into continental crust by plate collisions. Because the Canadian ophiolites were of Paleozoic age, the geologists suspected they were studying rocks formed by a plate collision that occurred before the existence of Pangaea. In studying the ophiolites, Canadian geophysicist J. Tuzo Wilson was led to wonder, "Did the Atlantic Ocean open, close, and then reopen?" Other geologists pondered the same question, piecing together data that suggest the following continental movements.

Precambrian Continents. Geological evidence indicates that the Atlantic and other oceans did open more than once along rift zones and that the continents have wandered substantially during the earth's history. In the earth's first 2 billion years, heat flow was three times greater within the earth than it is today, and mantle flow was extremely turbulent. Surface upheaval was violent. The crust was thinner and more unstable than at present, with scattered blocks, or "rockbergs," of granitic or continental crust embedded in basaltic or oceanic crust.

Very little continental crust was generated until about 4 billion years ago, when slices of granitic crust combined into larger bodies of highly altered granite, metamorphosed marine sediment, and lava flows, collectively known

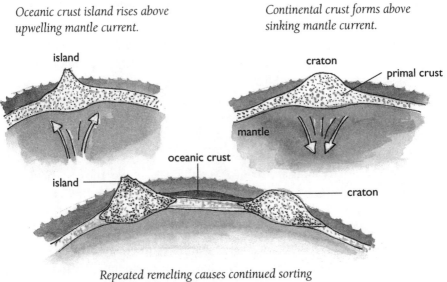

Oceanic crust island rises above upwelling mantle current.

Continental crust forms above sinking mantle current.

island

craton

primal crust

mantle

island

oceanic crust

craton

Repeated remelting causes continued sorting of crust into oceanic and continental.

Cratons, the nuclei of today's continents, formed during the Precambrian Era, 4 billion years ago.

Craton exposures throughout the world are low-lying expanses of basement rock called shields.

as basement rock. These bodies of Precambrian basement rock form the nuclei, or cratons, of all the world's continents. During the Precambrian, the cratons were small, independent ancestral continents, very mobile, that freewheeled over the earth's surface and occasionally collided. When crustal movement slowed considerably, by about 2 billion years ago, the pieces of granitic crust tended to stick together after collision rather than breaking away and wandering off again. The North American and other continents of 2 billion years ago managed to accumulate additional crust at the edges of their cratons and so grow larger. The cratons still form the hearts of the continents and, where exposed, are broad, low-lying exposures of basement rock called shields. One well-known shield, the Canadian Shield, is only one of seven crustal pieces that assembled the craton of North America.

By the late Precambrian, about 750 million years ago, the continents were at about their present sizes and had joined into a single landmass. That first known landmass was probably positioned over one of the poles, where intense glaciation occurred.

Paleozoic Continents. Between 750 and 550 million years ago, the ancestral landmass broke up. Pieces of the landmass reassembled into two mega-continents: Gondwana and Laurasia (named for Suess's Gondwanaland and Laurasia). Laurasia, in the Northern Hemisphere, included landmasses that are now North America, Greenland, Europe, and Asia. Gondwana comprised today's Africa, South America, Australia, Antarctica, and India. Later, India would

creation of a continent

As an ocean basin closes through the movement of landmasses, oceanic crust subducts beneath continental crust. Magma wells up, forming volcanoes on the overriding plate.

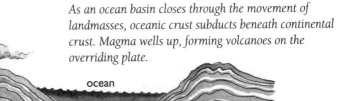

ocean

sediment

The ocean narrows. Subduction accelerates, and its accompanying volcanic and earthquake activity increases.

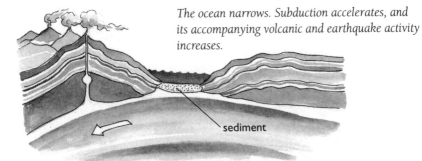

sediment

The ocean closes, and the continents collide. Oceanic crust deforms, and sediment is crammed against both continents.

oceanic crust

The two continents merge into one.

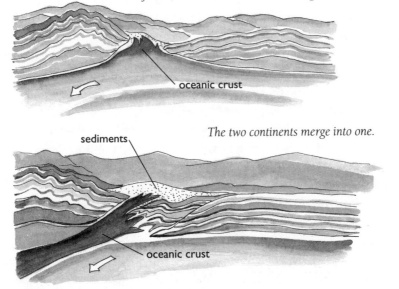

sediments

oceanic crust

break away, a subcontinent drifting north to southern Asia. The collision of subcontinent and continent would push up crust and create the Himalayas.

Gondwana and Laurasia were separated by a large ocean called the Tethys Sea. By the end of the Paleozoic Era, 240 million years ago, Gondwana and Laurasia had joined into the supercontinent known as Pangaea, which reached nearly from pole to pole. The rest of the globe was covered by a great sea known as Panthalassa. The closing of the Tethys Sea by plate movement joining Gondwana and Laurasia squeezed and uplifted the ocean floor and its accumulated sediments, forming the Ouachita and Appalachian Mountains of North America and the Hercynian Mountains of southern Europe. All are considered ancient mountain chains. All contain ophiolite complexes like those found in Canada in the 1960s, evidence of the massive plate collision that built seams of mountains across Pangaea.

Mesozoic Continents. The Mesozoic Era, 240 to 65 million years ago, saw the breakup and drifting of the continents toward their present positions. This time of vigorous tectonic activity was accompanied by much volcanism and deposition of great amounts of red sediments in today's Europe and North America, such as in deposits now found in the colorful Colorado Plateau. North and South America separated from each other, later moving west together from Europe and Africa as today's Atlantic Ocean opened. By the end of the Cretaceous, 65 million years ago, North America and Europe were joined only by a land bridge through Greenland. South America and Africa were separated by more than a thousand miles (more than 1,600 kilometers) of ocean. The Bering Strait between Alaska and Asia had narrowed. India was still traveling north to Asia, and Africa had separated from Antarctica and Australia.

Cenozoic Continents. Intense volcanism related to plate collision and movement continued into geology's modern age, the Cenozoic Era. With the continents nearly in their present positions, tectonic forces continued to drive terrain building, forming today's visible geologic features. The Rocky Mountains, stretching from Mexico to Canada, were pushed up between 80 and 40 million years ago, and the western United States' Basin and Range province developed, a series of north-south mountains separated by valleys. Rifting in both Mexico and Arabia separated peninsulas of land from their mainlands by opening the Gulf of California and the Red Sea. Antarctica and Australia broke away from South America, to which they had been connected by a narrow land bridge, and separated from each other. Antarctica moved south to the South Pole, where it acquired its thick ice cap; Australia moved northeast to its position in the Pacific Ocean.

Although no humans witnessed continental movement in the days of Pangaea, or even when Australia broke with Antarctica, we believe we are observing it today—in newly rifted rock material brought up in drill cores from the ocean floor, in volcanic activity and crust driving skyward at the edges of continents, in the earthquakes that release plate-driving pressures from deep in the earth. Continental drift remains a theory, however, one that best fits growing evidence from all over the world. We have only the rocks to go by. Evidence is still being pieced together, and there are gaps in our knowledge of the earth that have yet to be filled, but our search for understanding earth history is much of the fun of studying geology.

TO DO

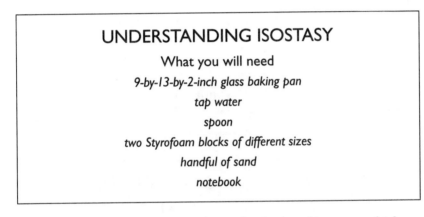

UNDERSTANDING ISOSTASY

What you will need

9-by-13-by-2-inch glass baking pan

tap water

spoon

two Styrofoam blocks of different sizes

handful of sand

notebook

One of geology's interesting principles is the theory of isostasy, which states that crustal plates of different sizes and densities will balance in the underlying mantle like icebergs in the ocean. The following activity demonstrates the concept of isostasy.

Fill the pan with water, and place the two Styrofoam blocks on the water. Sketch their appearance as they float side by side. Scoop a few teaspoonfuls of sand onto one of the blocks. Note the changes in your notebook. Next, scoop sand from the sandy block onto the other, and note how both readjust in the water. Your sketches of each stage of the experiment will help not only in your observations but also in answering questions about isostasy.

Explanation: The theory of isostasy says that the earth's crust "floats" on denser material, maintaining a state of equilibrium. Isostasy is achieved in part because of density differences between continental and oceanic crust and the underlying mantle. Picture an iceberg out at sea: The ice floats with about three-quarters of its mass below the water. One-quarter floats above, because the ice is less dense than the water. An iceberg twice as large as another is certain to have twice the mass underwater as well. Similarly, continents rise above the floors of oceanic crust because they are composed of less-dense rocks. Where the continental crust is quite thick, such as in mountainous regions, roots of the lighter crust are also large and extend down into underlying, denser material.

You began your experiment with Styrofoam "plates" of similar size and composition. When you deposited sand on one, you effectively increased the height of the plate and the size of its root. Although the sandfree plate had a lower surface, its root did not extend down as far. When you balanced the sand between the two, the plates again sought equilibrium, as the earth's crustal plates seek isostatic balance through similar adjustments.

If sediments are removed from a mountainous region by erosion and are deposited in an adjacent shallow sea, the areas become out of balance. The mountainous crust will slowly rise and the oceanic crust will sink as the underlying plastic mantle adjusts to the new conditions. You demonstrated the effects of erosion and redeposition by redistributing the sand with your spoon. What would happen to the continents if they did not rise after erosion? What isostatic adjustment must a continent make when it is covered with a large continental glacier? What must happen when the glacier melts?

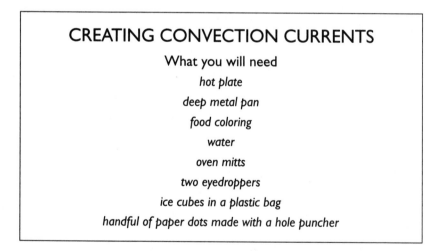

CREATING CONVECTION CURRENTS

What you will need

hot plate

deep metal pan

food coloring

water

oven mitts

two eyedroppers

ice cubes in a plastic bag

handful of paper dots made with a hole puncher

The circulation of the earth's heat in patterns that drive the crustal plates on the mantle is known as convection, a process easily illustrated with water and food coloring.

Fill the metal pan with water to within an inch (2.5 centimeters) of the top. Place the left edge of the pan on the hot plate, propping up the overhanging right edge with another pan or wooden blocks. Be sure to allow enough space around the hot plate to prevent fire danger. Place the bag of ice against the right side of the metal pan. Note that the pan will become partly hot and partly cold, so be sure to use your oven mitts. Use one eyedropper for blue food coloring and one for red. Drop three drops of blue into the water on the cold side and three drops of red on the hot side. Observe what happens to the colors, where they go when the currents reach the sides of the pan. Carefully sprinkle paper dots onto the water surface. Observe where they go and how they behave when they reach the edge of the pan.

Explanation: The water represents the mantle, and its flow in response to differences in temperature represents convection currents within the mantle. Think of the paper dots as crust, lighter material floating on denser moving material. Crustal plates are transported on denser mantle material in response to convection currents within the mantle. When currents reach the edge of their cycle, they dive down, forming circular patterns called convection cells.

RECONSTRUCTING PANGAEA

What you will need

scissors

tape

glue

crayons

continental puzzle pieces

light cardboard

Make a model of the world's most recent supercontinent using the puzzle pieces provided on the next page.

Trace the puzzle pieces onto a piece of paper. Glue the pieces to the cardboard and let dry. Cut out the puzzle pieces. Arrange them into one large landmass. You can stop there, or you can go on and demonstrate other continental movements. Study the illustration of rearranged continents in this chapter and references such as those listed in "To Read." Move the puzzle pieces to simulate each stage in continental movement. Note any rift zones, mountain chains, and features that can be traced across oceans. Demonstrate the opening of the Tethys Sea. Note the dates of continental convergence and separation. Where are the gaps in coastlines, and why do they exist? Where are the poles and equator for each configuration of continents?

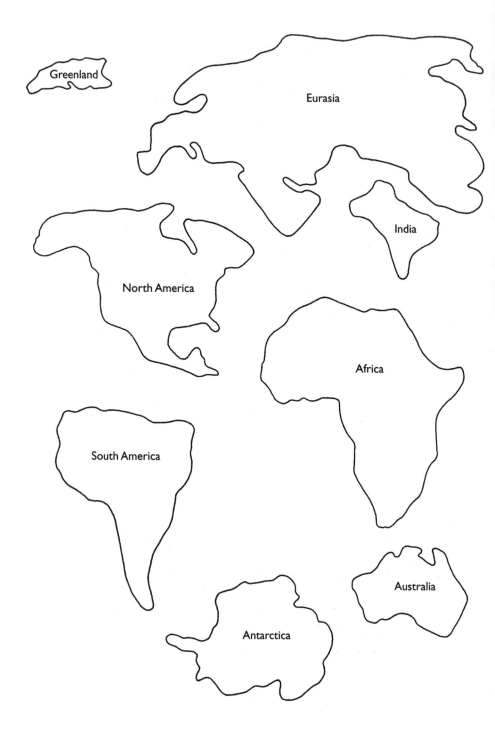

Explanation: You should be able to reconstruct not only Pangaea but also Gondwana and Laurasia. Scientists believe that the continents have maintained their present masses since around the beginning of the Paleozoic Era, between 750 and 550 million years ago, when the ancestral landmass broke up. Where continents do not mesh exactly is where erosion probably has caused relatively minor changes in continental outlines. Early scientific thought with respect to continental drift was that the continents never could have traveled such huge distances without their shapes having been greatly altered by erosive forces. Now such forces are believed to be small compared with tectonic forces.

TO THINK ABOUT

Dinosaurs in Isolation. One of the richest regions in the world for digging up fossil dinosaurs is the Gobi Desert in Mongolia, northwest of the Great Wall of China. The Gobi encompasses almost 500,000 square miles (1,295,000 square kilometers) of mainly uninhabited, arid land. In the 1920s, an expedition of American Museum of Natural History scientists traveled to the Gobi, led by Roy Chapman Andrews, whose team of paleontologists unearthed the first known dinosaur eggs, as well as previously unknown species of dinosaurs and ancient mammals. Andrews's successful expedition was to be the last of its kind for sixty years, however—from the 1920s to 1990, Mongolia was closed to teams of scientists from the west. Although other important paleontological expeditions from Russia, Poland, and Mongolia excavated dinosaurs in the Gobi after Andrews, their teams did not come close to exhausting all the fossil localities in the region. The Gobi is too large, remote, and inhospitable to travel to have been picked clean.

Because of their isolation, rich pockets of dinosaur fossils still remain in the Gobi, as was demonstrated by an international team of paleontologists from the American Museum and the Mongolian Academy of Sciences in the early 1990s. The paleontologists unearthed new types of fossils, including eggs containing evidence of the first-known embryos of meat-eating dinosaurs and previously undiscovered fragile skeletons of birdlike dinosaurs.

Another kind of isolation may have influenced dinosaurs in the Gobi as well. As we have seen, scientists who proposed the early theories of continental drift did so when they noticed that similar species of plants and animals appeared in the fossil record on widely separate continents. In the case of the Gobi dinosaurs, however, it has been suggested that the uniqueness of species, rather than similarities, are clues to continental drift. The Gobi dinosaurs may be different from their western counterparts because of the isolation that resulted when continental drift separated the area from other continents.

TO READ

Andrews, Roy Chapman. *This Business of Exploring.* New York: G. P. Putnam's Sons, 1935. This book explains more about the Gobi dinosaurs.

Erickson, Jon. *Plate Tectonics: Unraveling the Mysteries of the Earth.* New York: Facts on File, 1992. Part of The Changing Earth Series, this book covers most aspects of plate tectonics and has both clear text and illustrations.

Miller, Russell, and the editors of Time-Life Books. *Continents in Collision.* Alexandria, VA: Time-Life Books, 1982. A history of continental drift, with excellent illustrations.

Novacek, Michael. *Dinosaurs of the Flaming Cliffs.* New York: Doubleday, 1996. Another reference on Gobi dinosaurs.

TO WATCH

Earthquakes and Moving Continents. E. A. Video, 1991. This videotape, part of the special collection library at the United States Geological Survey, is for students in grades six through eight.

Exotic Terrane. United States Geological Survey–United States Forest Service, 1992. A geologic history of the Pacific Northwest region of the United States, illustrating how crust from across the Pacific Ocean moved and welded onto North America.

Geology. E. A. Video, 1991. This educational videotape, another in the special collection library at the United States Geological Survey, includes a unit on plate tectonics for students in grades four through six.

Tibet: Where Continents Collide, Part I. Earth Vision, 1989. Describes the geology and plate tectonics of the collision zone between India and Asia.

Understanding: Magnetism. Assignment Discovery Series. Discovery Channel, 1996. Samples from various layers of stone indicate that the earth's magnetic field has moved many times in the past but has kept its current magnetic alignment for seven hundred thousand years.

CHAPTER 9

Earthquakes: The Earth's Faults

Just after 5:00 A.M. on April 19, 1906, a major earthquake shook residents of San Francisco, California, awake from slumber. The ground shaking lasted only sixty-seven seconds, according to official records, but in that time many buildings collapsed, most water mains were damaged, and fires broke out throughout the city. Buildings constructed on bedrock were less susceptible to damage from ground shaking than those built on sediment, but the fires that burned out of control for days following the earthquake destroyed even those buildings that had withstood the initial shock. In the end, when the fires had been extinguished and the rubble of buildings was cleared, more than seven hundred people lay dead, and material losses exceeded $400 million (in today's dollars, probably over $2 billion). Even towns over 90 miles (150 kilometers) distant were damaged severely, and massive landslides were released in nearby mountains.

CAUSES OF EARTHQUAKES

The 1906 earthquake in San Francisco is not the largest or most destructive earthquake on record for the twentieth century, but it is especially significant for one reason: Because of geologic observation conducted in the area directly afterward, the 1906 earthquake began our understanding of the natural forces that caused it. Historical records since before the time of Christ describe great shaking of the ground, accounts interpreted by scholars to be descriptions of earthquakes. But not until the studies of 1906 did we recognize that earthquakes are caused by slippage along faults, or breaks in the earth's crust. That recognition allowed scientists to view earthquakes in a new light—the slippage could be measured and earthquakes described quantitatively.

The study that followed the 1906 earthquake, conducted by Harry F. Reid of Johns Hopkins University, found as much as 6.5 yards (6 meters) of offset, or displacement, in fences and roads crossing the San Andreas fault, a major fault along the North American coast. The San Andreas fault is understood to represent a generally vertical plane at the meeting of the Pacific and North American tectonic plates. In addition to the Reid study, measurements taken before and after the occurrence of the earthquake indicated that the rocks near the fault had been broken and offset. From his observations, Reid came up with the elastic-rebound theory of earthquake generation. The theory

Evidence from the 1906 San Francisco earthquake. This fence near Point Reyes, California, was displaced 8.5 feet (2.5 meters) across the San Andreas fault.

the San Andreas fault

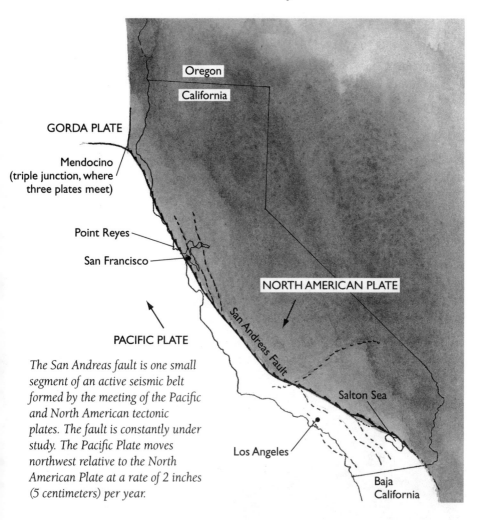

Oregon

California

GORDA PLATE

Mendocino
(triple junction, where
three plates meet)

Point Reyes

San Francisco

NORTH AMERICAN PLATE

San Andreas Fault

PACIFIC PLATE

Salton Sea

Los Angeles

Baja
California

The San Andreas fault is one small segment of an active seismic belt formed by the meeting of the Pacific and North American tectonic plates. The fault is constantly under study. The Pacific Plate moves northwest relative to the North American Plate at a rate of 2 inches (5 centimeters) per year.

states that rocks behave elastically—they are capable of recovering size and shape after being deformed or strained. Mechanical energy can be stored in them for later release, the same way it is stored in a compressed spring. When two rock masses on opposite sides of a fault strain in different directions, they cannot move because of friction, and energy is stored. When the energy builds up enough to overcome friction, the rocks break at their weakest point. They spring back to an equilibrium state. The elastic rebound, or springing back, releases energy in the form of heat generated by the movement and as earthquake, or seismic, waves.

the elastic rebound theory of earthquake generation

pre-quake   post-quake

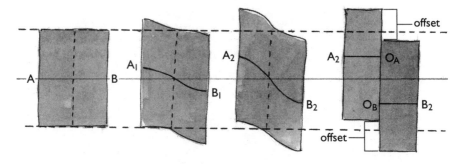

Before an earthquake begins, rocks lie on opposite sides of an incipient fault.

As strain begins in opposite directions across the fault, rocks are distorted, but no slippage occurs along the fault.

Energy is stored in the deformed rock, still without movement on the fault.

Release of energy in an earthquake causes slippage along the fault line, allowing rocks to recover original sizes and shapes but with offset across the fault.

elastic rebound of the earth's crust

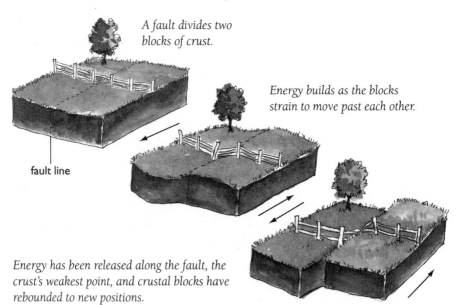

A fault divides two blocks of crust.

Energy builds as the blocks strain to move past each other.

fault line

Energy has been released along the fault, the crust's weakest point, and crustal blocks have rebounded to new positions.

Other mechanisms besides elastic rebound may be at work during earthquakes as well. Research performed since Reid's studies suggests that in some places along faults, the forces holding two fault blocks together is stronger than the rock itself. In such cases, ruptures occur in other places besides directly along the fault. In some instances, fault movement occurs after earthquakes take place. But geologists agree that faults exist and movement along them occurs. Along faults like the San Andreas, a surface expression of the seam between two large crustal plates, the associated earthquakes are called tectonic—the largest and most destructive of earthquakes.

DISTRIBUTION OF EARTHQUAKES

Because they are largely associated with the meeting of crustal plates, earthquakes, like volcanoes, tend to occur along well-defined belts. Approximately 80 percent of the world's earthquakes manifest along the edges of the Pacific Plate, creating a circum-Pacific belt that extends from Chile in South America, up along the western edge of North America, north to the Aleutian Islands, west to Japan, and south to the Philippines, Indonesia, New Zealand, and some Pacific Islands. Approximately 15 percent of the world's earthquakes occur along a second major seismic belt, the Mediterranean and Trans-Asiatic belt, extending from the Mediterranean area through the Himalayas and Alps

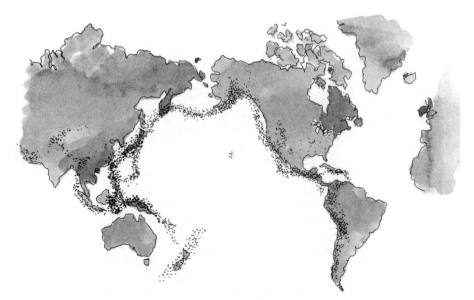

The world's most active seismic belt rings the Pacific Ocean, along the edges of the Pacific Plate.

and including Spain, Italy, Greece, and northern India. Another 5 percent of earthquakes occur in parts of the world besides the two major seismic belts.

RECORDING EARTHQUAKES

When rocks break and spring back to new positions, vibrations are generated through the ground. The vibrations are of two basic types: compression waves and shear waves. They are generated at the focus of the earthquake, the point in the earth where the vibrations begin. From the focus, the waves radiate outward, becoming weaker with distance traveled.

Compression waves, or P waves, travel longitudinally through the deep interior of the earth at speeds of 3.4 to 8.6 miles (5.5 to 13.8 kilometers) per second. People experiencing the shaking of an earthquake feel the vibrations of the P waves first, as a sharp thud or shock. A few seconds later, the slower shear waves, or S waves, arrive, traveling at 2.2 to 4.5 miles (3.5 to 7.1 kilometers) per second, setting up a swaying or rolling motion that can be seen in the wavelike action of the ground, concrete, and other surfaces affected by the waves. Earthquake research stations, such as the National Earthquake Information Service in Golden, Colorado, use seismographs to record the arrival of seismic waves. A seismograph consists of a pendulum and a recording

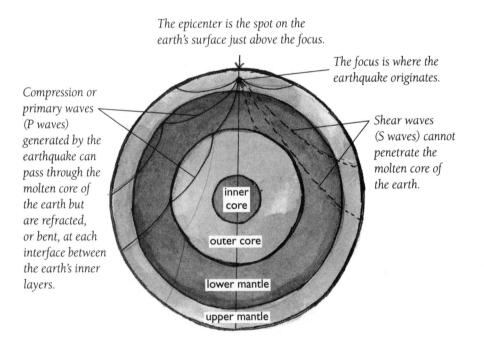

The epicenter is the spot on the earth's surface just above the focus.

The focus is where the earthquake originates.

Compression or primary waves (P waves) generated by the earthquake can pass through the molten core of the earth but are refracted, or bent, at each interface between the earth's inner layers.

Shear waves (S waves) cannot penetrate the molten core of the earth.

inner core

outer core

lower mantle

upper mantle

device such as a drum of graph paper operated by clockwork. The pendulum is attached to a frame embedded in bedrock, swinging freely and moved by waves while the rest of the seismograph is rigidly attached. When the crust is not moving, the seismograph will record a flat line. When earthquake waves are registered, they are recorded as wavy lines on the seismograph. By comparing the travel times of P and S waves to the seismograph, geologists measure the distance to the earthquake's epicenter, the point on the surface of the earth directly above the earthquake's focus.

MEASURING EARTHQUAKES

The size of an earthquake is measured by two parameters: magnitude and intensity.

Magnitude. Magnitude is a measure of how much energy is released during an earthquake. Sometimes seismic energy is released quickly and violently, when large portions of faults slip past each other in seconds. Sometimes energy is released slowly and more benignly, when portions of a fault creep past each other over many years, never building huge amounts of strain. The release of energy as recorded by seismographs is measured on the Richter scale, which was developed in the 1930s and 1940s by Charles F. Richter and Beno Gutenberg of the California Institute of Technology. The Richter scale describes earthquake magnitude on a scale of 1 to 10. Each larger number on the scale equals ten times the value of the previous number. Earthquakes of magnitude 7 or greater are considered major. Magnitude 8 or larger constitutes a great earthquake. In the twentieth century, more than 50 earthquakes have been measured as great. Some examples in recent history are the Gansu, China, earthquake of 1920 (magnitude 8.6); the Tangshan, China, earthquake of 1976 (magnitude 8.2); and the Mexico City earthquake of 1985 (magnitude 8.1). In each of these earthquakes, deaths ranged from tens of thousands to hundreds of thousands, and large portions of cities were destroyed.

San Francisco's 1906 earthquake registered magnitude 8.3 on the Richter scale, as did Alaska's Good Friday earthquake in 1964. Scientists judged the Alaskan earthquake to have released one hundred times more energy than the San Francisco earthquake, however, leading to the suspicion that the Richter scale is inaccurate at its upper end. We understand now that the scale becomes saturated by large earthquakes in which waves are emitted by ruptures of very long faults. To measure the energy released by such earthquakes, researchers developed another scale that uses seismic moment. The seismic moment measures the seismic energy emitted from an entire fault rather than just a portion of it. On the seismic moment scale, San Francisco's earthquake

Modified Mercalli Intensity Scale of 1931

I — Not felt by people, except under especially favorable circumstances. However, dizziness or nausea may be experienced.

> Sometimes birds and animals are uneasy or disturbed. Trees, structures, liquids, and bodies of water may sway gently, and doors may swing very slowly.

II — Felt indoors by a few people, especially on upper floors of multi-story buildings, and by sensitive or nervous persons.

> As in Grade I, birds and animals are disturbed, and trees, structures, liquids, and bodies of water may sway. Hanging objects swing, especially if they are delicately suspended.

III — Felt indoors by several people, usually as a rapid vibration that may not be recognized as an earthquake at first. Vibration is similar to that of lightly loaded trucks, or heavy trucks some distance away. Duration may be estimated in some cases.

> Movements may be appreciable on upper levels of tall structures. Standing motor cars may rock slightly.

IV — Felt indoors by many, outdoors by few. Awakens a few individuals, particularly light sleepers, but frightens no one except those apprehensive from previous experience. Vibration like that due to passing of heavy or heavily loaded trucks. Sensation like a heavy body striking a building, or the falling of heavy objects inside.

> Dishes, windows, and doors rattle; glassware and crockery clink and clash. Walls and house frames creak, especially if intensity is in the upper range of this grade. Hanging objects often swing. Liquids in open vessels are disturbed slightly. Stationary automobiles rock noticeably.

V — Felt indoors by practically everyone, outdoors by most people. Direction can often be estimated by those outdoors. Awakens many, or most sleepers. Frightens a few people, with slight excitement; some persons run outdoors.

> Buildings tremble throughout. Dishes and glassware break to some extent. Windows crack in some cases, but not generally. Vases and small or unstable objects overturn in many instances, and a few fall. Hanging objects and doors swing generally or considerably. Pictures knock against walls, or swing out of place. Doors and shutters open or close abruptly. Pendulum clocks stop, or run fast or slow. Small objects move, and furnishings may shift to a slight extent. Small amounts of liquids spill from well-filled open containers. Trees and bushes shake slightly.

VI — Felt by everyone, indoors and outdoors. Awakens all sleepers. Frightens many people; general excitement; some persons run outdoors.

> Persons move unsteadily. Trees and bushes shake slightly to moderately. Liquids are set in strong motion. Small bells in churches and schools ring. Poorly built buildings may be damaged. Plaster falls in small amounts. Other plaster cracks somewhat. Many dishes and glasses, and a few windows, break. Knick-knacks, books, and pictures fall. Furniture overturns in many instances. Heavy furnishings move.

VII — Frightens everyone. General alarm. Everyone runs outdoors.

> People find it difficult to stand. Persons driving cars notice shaking. Trees and bushes shake moderately to strongly. Waves form on ponds, lakes and streams. Water is muddied. Gravel or sand stream banks cave in. Large church bells ring. Suspended objects quiver. Damage is negligible in buildings of good design and construction; slight to moderate in well-built ordinary buildings; considerable in poorly built or badly designed buildings, adobe houses, old walls (especially where laid up without mortar), spires, etc. Plaster and some stucco fall. Many windows and some furniture breaks. Loosened brickwork and tiles shake down. Weak chimneys break at the roof line. Cornices fall

from towers and high buildings. Bricks and stones are dislodged. Heavy furniture overturns. Concrete irrigation ditches are considerably damaged.

VIII General fright, and alarm approaches panic.

Persons driving cars are disturbed. Trees shake strongly, and branches and trunks break off (especially palm trees). Sand and mud erupts in small amounts. Flow of springs and wells is temporarily and sometimes permanently changed. Dry wells renew flow. Temperatures of spring and well waters vary. Damage slight in brick structures built especially to withstand earthquakes; considerable in ordinary substantial buildings, with some partial collapse; heavy in some wooden houses, with some tumbling down. Panel walls break away in frame structures. Decayed pilings break off. Walls fall. Solid stone walls crack and break seriously. Wet grounds and steep slopes crack to some extent. Chimneys, columns, monuments, and factory stacks and towers twist and fall. Very heavy furniture moves conspicuously or overturns.

IX Panic is general.

Ground cracks conspicuously. Damage is considerable in masonry structures built especially to withstand earthquakes; great in other masonry buildings—some collapse in large part. Some wood frame houses built especially to withstand earthquakes are thrown out of plumb; others are shifted wholly off foundations. Reservoirs are seriously damaged and underground pipes sometimes break.

X Panic is general.

Ground, especially when loose and wet, cracks up to widths of several inches; fissures up to a yard in width run parallel to canal and stream bands. Landsliding is considerable from river banks and steep coasts. Sand and mud shifts horizontally on beaches and flat land. Water level changes in wells. Water is thrown on banks of canals, lakes, rivers, etc. Dams, dikes, and embankments are seriously damaged. Well-built wooden structures and bridges are severely damaged, and some collapse. Dangerous cracks develop in excellent brick walls. Most masonry and frame structures, and their foundations, are destroyed. Railroad rails bend slightly. Pipelines buried in earth tear apart or are crushed endwise. Wide cracks and broad, wavy folds open in cement pavements and asphalt road surfaces.

XI Panic is general.

Disturbances in ground are many and widespread, varying with the ground material. Broad fissures, earth slumps, and landslides develop in soft, wet ground. Water charged with sand and mud is ejected in large amounts. Sea waves of significant magnitude may develop. Damage is severe to wood frame structures, especially near shock centers, and great to dams, dikes, and embankments, even at long distances. Few if any masonry structures remain standing. Supporting piers or pillars of large, well-built bridges are wrecked. Wooden bridges with some flexibility are less affected. Railroad rails bend greatly, and some are thrust endwise. Pipelines buried in earth are put completely out of service.

XII Panic is general.

Damage is total, and practically all works of construction are damaged greatly or destroyed. Disturbances in the ground are great and varied, and numerous shearing cracks develop. Landslides, rock falls, and slumps in river banks are numerous and extensive. Large rock masses are wrenched loose and torn off. Fault slips develop in form rock, and horizontal and vertical offset displacements are notable. Water channels, both surface and underground, are disturbed and modified greatly. Lakes are dammed, new waterfalls are produced, rivers are deflected, etc. Surface waves are seen on ground surfaces. Lines of sight are distorted. Objects are thrown upward into the air.

registered 7.9, Alaska's 9.2. In 1966, Keiiti Aki of the Massachusetts of Technology demonstrated that the seismic moment is determined not only by the rupture size but also by the average slip of the fault and how rigid the faulted material is. So the difference in seismic moment between the San Francisco and Alaskan earthquakes was probably due to a combination of factors: differences in rock and soil in the two areas, size of the ruptures, and distance moved along the faults.

The strongest earthquake on record on the seismic moment scale is the Chilean earthquake of 1960, which measured 9.5. Both the Chilean and Alaskan earthquakes generated tsunamis, huge ocean waves that swept inland to destroy property and cause loss of life. In the case of Chile, the tsunamis ranged in height from 12 to 30 feet (3.5 to 9 meters), destroying several villages in Chile and then sweeping across the Pacific Ocean as quickly as 450 miles (more than 700 kilometers) an hour to ruin villages in Hawaii and Japan. The magnitude of such great earthquakes can be described well only by the seismic moment scale.

Intensity. The second measure of an earthquake's size is intensity, the amount of physical damage or geologic change brought about by the ground shaking. Damage is most intense closest to an earthquake's epicenter. One measure of intensity is the modified Mercalli scale, in which intensity is expressed in Roman numerals from I to XII. An earthquake of intensity II is barely felt by most people in the area of ground shaking; an earthquake of intensity VI is felt by all; an earthquake of intensity X causes heavy damage, including destruction of wooden structures and masonry, cracking of ground, and landslides on steep nearby slopes.

LIVING WITH EARTHQUAKES

Earthquakes are inevitable on our planet, but high death tolls and huge amounts of property loss can be decreased through intelligent planning and design. Scientists recommend proper building construction in earthquake country, selective land use, and accurate earthquake prediction as means of reducing loss due to ground shaking. The first strategy, proper building construction in areas prone to earthquakes, has become obvious through painful experience. The 1976 Tangshan earthquake killed 242,000 people, largely due to the collapse of buildings constructed of stacked concrete slabs. Expected damage to light metal frame and wooden frame buildings is much less than to those constructed of concrete and masonry, a fact that should be reflected in building codes in earthquake-prone areas.

Intelligent land use with regard to earthquakes is essential. Ground shaking is much greater in soft soils than in bedrock, as illustrated by the 1985 Mexico City earthquake, which caused severe ground shaking and liquefaction in water-saturated sediments in part of the city built on landfill. In the 1989 Loma Prieta earthquake in the San Francisco Bay area, the collapse of the Cypress Viaduct and damage to the Bay Bridge resulted from the shaking of underlying soft soils, which magnified the earthquake's effects. Special engineering design and restrictions on the use of fill beneath structures in earthquake country will help prevent similar tragedies.

The third preventive strategy, earthquake prediction, is still in its infancy. Geologists can tell which portions of faults are prone to rupturing, but not necessarily when such rupturing will occur. The best we can do to date is to use a seismic warning system such as the seismic alarms in use in Mexico City. Although not always reliable, the alarms give residents fifty seconds of warning time to evacuate buildings. Long- and short-term warnings, as well as emergency planning and intelligent design, give residents in areas prone to earthquakes some measure of defense and sense of security.

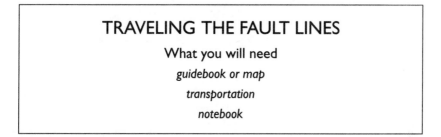

TO DO

TRAVELING THE FAULT LINES

What you will need

guidebook or map

transportation

notebook

Search in the field for the surface expressions of faults and the damage caused by earthquakes.

First, select a guide to the earthquake country you wish to visit. Not all areas of the world are in active earthquake zones; make sure your search for field features is within an area of active seismicity. It helps to have a good guidebook. Several guidebooks apply to the much-studied San Andreas fault in California (two are listed under "To Read" at the end of this chapter). Follow the leads of the guidebooks. In the earthquake area, look for signs of fault movement by checking for laterally offset features, sag ponds, oases, fault scarps, offset beds in roadcuts, and offset streams.

field features to look for when watching for faults

Sag ponds form when runoff water is trapped in little basins along a fault. The sag ponds in this drawing border a fault scarp, the steep ridge or cliff resulting from sudden vertical movement along a fault line. Erosion has softened the edges and base of this scarp.

Streams of the Carrizo Plain of California. The streams cut across a fault and were subsequently offset by its movement.

Classic palm oases can develop in arid regions where underground water approaches the surface along faults.

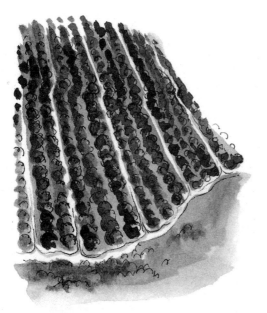

Other linear features are excellent indicators of fault movement, as in this orange grove in the Imperial Valley, California. Displacement here occurred suddenly after a 7.1-magnitude earthquake on May 18, 1940.

Explanation: By following directions to fault features and studying them, you can spot them when traveling elsewhere. Refer to your notes and drawings, and you can create your own guide to less explored faulted areas.

MODELING EARTHQUAKE WAVES

What you will need

long coiled spring or Slinky

yarn

Recruit a partner to help demonstrate how P and S waves travel through a medium.

Tie a small length of yarn to every tenth coil of spring. Holding both ends of the spring, rest it on a counter top or tabletop. Then stretch out the spring until you feel some tension. Ask your partner to hold the end of the spring firmly. Abruptly push your end toward your partner, then bring it quickly back into place. Observe the spring and the waves moving through it. Next, hold your end firmly and have your partner snap the spring from side to side. Observe the spring's movement.

In which direction did the first wave move? The second? Which wave

fault features

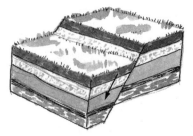

In a normal fault, pulling apart causes one block to slip down the fault face, or scarp, relative to the other block.

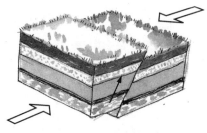

In a reverse fault, compression causes one block to move up the fault scarp relative to the other block.

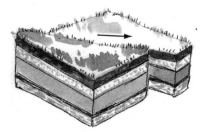

Movement along a lateral fault is horizontal. In a right lateral fault, horizontal movement of the block across the fault appears to be to the right.

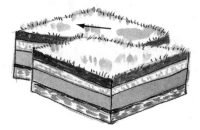

A left lateral fault shows apparent movement of the block across the fault to the left.

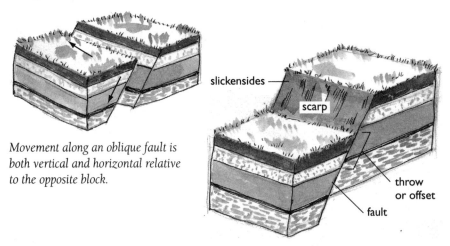

Movement along an oblique fault is both vertical and horizontal relative to the opposite block.

Slickensides, shiny scraped surfaces, often form on fault faces, or scarps. Offset is the amount of displacement across a fault. The fault itself is the plane along which movement occurs and that separates opposite crustal blocks. The lines drawn on the blocks represent corresponding sedimentary layers offset across the fault plane.

appeared to move more quickly? What happened to the yarn each time? Repeat several times and observe again.

Explanation: The first wave you generated was a P, or primary, wave. P waves create a push-pull effect in rocks. They travel faster than S, or shear, waves, which are the second waves you generated. S waves vibrate at right angles to the direction they travel. They create the swaying or rolling motion felt during an earthquake.

SLIPPING AWAY

What you will need
your hands

Use this simple experiment to gain a sense of opposite motion on fault lines.

Clench both fists. Bring them together with the knuckles at the center. Alternate the knuckle of one hand with the knuckle of the other, fitting them together mountain to valley. Apply pressure until they're snug. Then try to move your hands laterally, so that the knuckles move past each other. Not only does it hurt, but it's hard to do. When the knuckles do move, movement is abrupt and significant.

Explanation: If your fists were the earth's crust, this sudden movement would be the earthquake. The pressure you applied in trying to move your fists laterally was like the energy in the earth pushing crustal blocks in opposite directions. You can change the orientation of your fists (thumbs up, down, or sideways), but the problem remains: Movement along the central plane can be sporadic and sizable.

TO THINK ABOUT

Liquefaction. In dry sand, the network of sedimentary clasts supports the weight of overlying clasts and structures. When water is added to sand to the point of saturation, water fills pore spaces between clasts. The sand becomes loosely packed and can no longer hold the weight of overlying objects. When jolted, saturated sand or sediment flows like liquid, or liquefies, as the force of the impact is transferred to the water in the pore spaces. Saturated sediments such as sand are known to liquefy during the intense ground shaking caused by earthquakes. In the 1906 earthquake in San Francisco, areas built on fill, unconsolidated material brought in from elsewhere, sustained the worst damage to structures, roads, and rails.

Studies conducted in Alaska after the 1964 earthquake turned up interesting evidence of liquefaction along the Alaska Railroad. Wet soil in areas usually capable of supporting the railroad had liquefied during the earthquake. Material in stream canyons flowed downhill into valleys, warping the rails that crossed them; other sediment flowed from channel banks into the centers of streams, buckling bridges through compression. Other signs of liquefaction indicated that slides were set off from bluffs in Anchorage: Among residential neighborhoods perched above the ocean, ground shaking turned wet sand and clay into an oozing, moving mass that broke free and slid toward the sea. Seventy-five homes and the people inside tumbled down with the liquefied sediment.

Liquefaction of sediments probably also caused the intense disturbance of the Cypress Viaduct and the Bay Bridge during the 1989 Loma Prieta earthquake in the San Francisco Bay area. Other areas of fill surround the bay, many that are the sites of large neighborhoods. Geologists have warned against building structures on fill, where the material becomes saturated and prone to liquefaction. It is as important to understand the nature of the soil underlying a potential building site as it is to know where the faults lie in earthquake country.

TO READ

Ayer, Eleanor H. *Earthquake Country: Traveling California's Fault Lines.* Frederick, CO: Renaissance House, 1992. This little guide contains descriptions of historic earthquake destruction and provides street and field directions to fault-related features.

Iacopi, Robert. *Earthquake Country: How, Why, and Where Earthquakes Strike in California.* Menlo Park, CA: Lane Publishing Company, 1971. This Sunset Book is an excellent travel guide to field features caused by earthquakes in California.

Richter, Charles F. *Elementary Seismology.* New York: W. H. Freeman and Company, 1958. An authoritative reference on the causes of earthquakes by the codeveloper of the Richter scale.

Schulz, Sandra. *The San Andreas Fault.* Washington, DC: United States Government Printing Office, 1989. One of a series of general interest publications prepared by the United States Geological Survey.

Walker, Bryce, and the editors of Time-Life Books. *Earthquake.* Alexandria, VA: Time-Life Books, 1982. Great pictures and text fill this Planet Earth series book.

TO WATCH

Alaska Earthquake! Spirit of Survival Series. Discovery Channel, 1996. Examines the Good Friday earthquake of 1964 and associated tsunamis that killed 131 people and destroyed many of Alaska's cities.

The Alaskan Earthquake. United States Geological Survey, 1966. This film, taken before, during, and after the Alaskan earthquake, shows footage of the tsunamis and effects of coastal uplift, liquefaction, and fault movement.

Mapping Earthquakes. Seismology Lecture Series. University of California–Berkeley, 1989. Shows techniques for mapping the location and magnitude of earthquakes.

The Parkfield Earthquake Prediction Experiment: The Emergency Response. Open-File Report 88-504. United States Geological Survey, 1988. The story of Parkfield, a town on the San Andreas Fault, which is well situated for earthquake prediction and forecasting experiments.

Seismic Waves—Wave Properties. Seismology Lecture Series. University of California–Berkeley, 1989. Uses a hydraulic tank to generate waves in water and illustrate seismic wave properties.

When the Earth Quakes. National Geographic Television, 1990. Includes footage from the Alaskan earthquake of 1964 and the Loma Prieta earthquake of 1989.

CHAPTER 10

Planetary Geology: Rocks in Space

The big bang theory of the origin and evolution of the universe says that it was born in an instant. At one moment between 10 and 20 billion years ago, our universe existed only as a sort of embryo no bigger than the nucleus of an atom. The next moment, it was a hot primal system, exploding and expanding from the material it had contained. With time and further expansion, subatomic particles within the system united into atoms of hydrogen and helium and other light elements that gathered into huge clouds. Ultimately the clouds of matter collapsed from gravity into galaxies, independent collections of matter strewn through our universe.

In our particular galaxy, the Milky Way, the matter in our solar system hung together because of the pull of the primordial sun's gravity. Particles orbited the sun in a single plane, a flat disk spinning around a central globe. The disk must have resembled Saturn's rings, countless coarse particles known as planetesimals in elliptical orbit around the infant sun. The planetesimals

Bands of gas and dust particles orbit in a giant disk around the infant sun.

collided and joined, or accreted, forming larger bodies that eventually became the planets in our solar system.

As the sun reached a critical mass, it ignited and gave off a solar wind that blew lighter particles to the outer system. In the inner solar system, planetesimals were composed of stone and metal fragments. In the outer solar system, planetesimals were frozen water and carbon dioxide, crystalline methane, and condensed ammonia. Today, the composition of the planets reflects this early sorting of dense and light particles by solar wind. The inner planets in our solar system, the terrestrials—Mercury, Venus, Earth, and Mars—are small rocky worlds with metal cores. Four outer planets, the gas giants—Jupiter, Saturn, Uranus, and Neptune—are collections of gas and liquid centered around deep rock cores. The ninth and outermost planet, Pluto, seems to be mostly ice.

In the process of planetary accretion, dust and ice particles coalesced into larger particles, planetesimals, that continued colliding, shattering, and recombining.

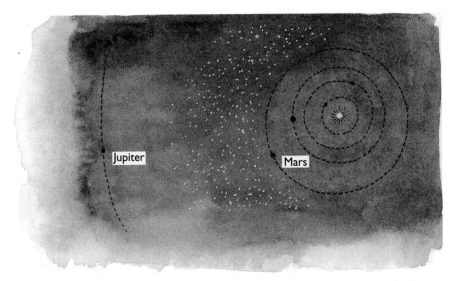

The wide band of asteroids orbiting the sun between Mars and Jupiter is believed to be a collection of planetesimals that never fully accreted.

Between the orbits of Mars and Jupiter lies the asteroid belt, a wide band of asteroids found between 142 and 485 million miles (230 and 780 million kilometers) from the sun. Current thinking is that the asteroids are planetesimals that were never allowed to coalesce into larger bodies, perhaps because of the gravitational influence of the giant Jupiter. The asteroid belt is not as dense as it once was; after colliding, asteroids in the belt either accrete or range on

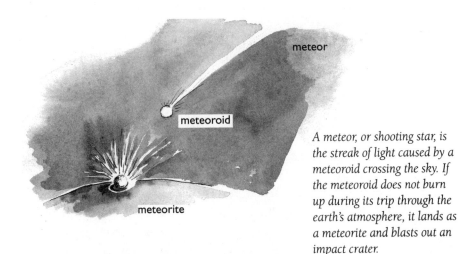

A meteor, or shooting star, is the streak of light caused by a meteoroid crossing the sky. If the meteoroid does not burn up during its trip through the earth's atmosphere, it lands as a meteorite and blasts out an impact crater.

A popular example of an impact crater is Meteor Crater (or Barringer Crater) near Winslow, Arizona. Created some fifty thousand years ago by a 100-foot (30-meter) diameter metallic asteroid, the crater is almost 1 mile (about 1.5 kilometer) across and 750 feet (225 meters) deep.

courses independent from the orbit between Mars and Jupiter. If then drawn by our sun's gravitational influence, the ranging asteroids move toward the inner planets, eventually to collide with one of them. If headed for earth, the smaller asteroids, known as meteoroids, often burn out in the earth's atmosphere, becoming bright streaks of light called meteors. Some meteoroids, especially if composed of metal, reach the earth, thereby earning the name meteorite. About fifty plum-sized meteorites hit the earth every day, rarely witnessed, sometimes recovered (most often, it seems, by farmers plowing large expanses of field). Larger meteorites, asteroids that have reached earth, are more rare. In some cases, however, impacts of large meteorites have changed the earth's geologic history significantly.

METEORITES

Scientists believe that meteoritic impacts were frequent and severe in the earth's early years. Today meteorites play a smaller part in the earth's history—as planetesimals accreted into planets in our solar system, their numbers decreased. Fewer are now free to become ranging asteroids. Between 4.2 and 3.8 billion years ago, however, asteroids both in and out of the belt were plentiful, and a shower of 50-mile (80-kilometer) wide meteorites bombarded the young earth and its new moon. The results were catastrophic: Meteorites penetrated the crust of both earth and moon, causing massive outpourings of basalt, creating magma oceans, and leaving huge impact craters. The moon, which has neither plate tectonic activity nor intense weather systems, still shows fresh impact craters on its surface. The earth's craters, on the other hand, are better hidden. They have been either subducted with oceanic crust in trenches or eroded by wind and water over billions of years.

Today, although major meteoritic collisions are infrequent, astronomers maintain a careful watch of asteroids (and comets, rare sun-orbiting visitors from beyond the orbit of Neptune) that penetrate our solar system deeper than Mars's orbit. Any asteroids that approach this closely are called near-earth asteroids; those 300 feet (about 100 meters) or larger in size are considered threatening to life on this planet. One near-earth asteroid, approximately 200 feet (about 60 meters) in diameter, exploded in the atmosphere above Siberia in 1908. Although the asteroid never reached the ground and its fragments did not cause cratering, the explosion laid waste to a 30-mile (50-kilometer) area. Its blast, which resembled a nuclear explosion, could be heard across Europe and in the United Kingdom.

Larger asteroids, 5 miles (about 10 kilometers) or more in diameter, collide with the earth approximately every 100 million years. Geologists debate whether one or more asteroids of this size collided with the earth 65 million years ago and destroyed the dinosaurs and most other life forms. Mounting evidence suggests that asteroids did impact the earth then—five candidate craters date back to the great Cretaceous-Tertiary boundary extinction. One in particular, a 110-mile (170-kilometer) diameter crater in the Yucatán Peninsula, Mexico, was identified from rock samples pulled up by geologists drilling for oil in the area, as well as from images taken by the space shuttle *Endeavour*. The Yucatán depression suggests the meteorite was 6 to 12 miles (10 to 20 kilometers) in diameter upon impact with the earth. The impact of a body that size would have torn a hole in the crust 100 miles (160 kilometers) wide,

High-pressure shock waves forced through the ground near impact craters mark quartz grains within rocks with distinctive parallel striations.

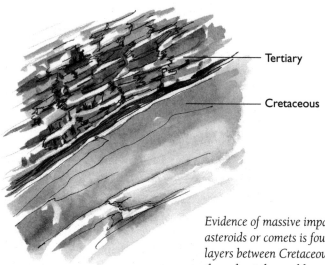

Tertiary

Cretaceous

Evidence of massive impact by one or more asteroids or comets is found in iridium-rich clay layers between Cretaceous and Tertiary strata throughout the world.

triggered enormous explosions, instigated worldwide earthquakes and tsunamis, and raised huge clouds of dust that blocked the sun and plunged the globe into a freezing darkness. Throughout the world, rocks of the Cretaceous-Tertiary boundary, such as those in the Yucatán crater, contain evidence of impact in shocked quartz grains, distinctive grains of quartz with striations caused by high-pressure shock waves; soot believed to come from global forest fires; and deposits of iridium, a rare isotope of platinum that is abundant on meteorites but usually scarce in the earth's crust. Ocean-floor drilling by an international team of scientists in early 1997 off the coast of Florida, about 1,000 miles (1,600 kilometers) from the Yucatan depression, turned up further evidence of an asteroidal impact sixty-five million years ago: Drill cores contain samples of rocks that indicate a healthy, teeming ocean, followed by four progressively younger layers believed to be unmistakable evidence of an impact. The first layer is a jumble of rubble from melted terrestrial rock thrown skyward, presumably by the impact; the second is the rusty debris of the asteroid itself; the third is a gray, clay "dead" layer; and the fourth shows an explosion of new life in a 2-to 4-inch (5- to 10-centimeter) thick layer that includes tiny but well-preserved fossils. Apparently the dead zone following the impact lasted only about 5,000 years, in which time the tiny organisms that survived the blast repopulated the oceans.

Scientists suspect that similar meteoritic impacts may have caused other major extinctions evident in the fossil record, such as the disappearance of nearly half the reptile families around 225 million years ago.

OTHER COLLISIONS

Some scientists believe that a meteoritic collision that occurred about 4.6 billion years ago was responsible for the formation of the earth's moon. The collision was so forceful that it tore a hole in the earth's crust. Material pouring from the mantle through the tear entered into orbit around the earth. In much the same way as the original planetesimals accreted into planets, the liberated earthly material merged to form our orbiting moon.

Rock samples collected from the moon by astronauts of the 1960s and 1970s Apollo missions corroborate this theory: The compositions of the rocks attest that they could have come from the earth's upper mantle. None is younger than 3.2 billion years old, suggesting that no new rock was made since the heavy volcanic activity that must have covered the moon shortly after its original molten material separated from earth.

Other early meteoritic impacts include collisions with shield rock in present-day Canada, Australia, and Africa during the formation of the cratons in the earth's first 2 billion years. In the areas suspected of impacts, some

A popular theory of our moon's formation involves collision of the earth with an asteroid. This drawing shows the earth after the collision, which tore a large hole in the earth's crust, allowing molten magma to pour out into space, forming a protolunar disk of debris. The moon increased in size as it gathered up debris in its orbit around the earth. Meteorites of rock fragments bombarded the moon's surface, creating the crater-pocked satellite we now see.

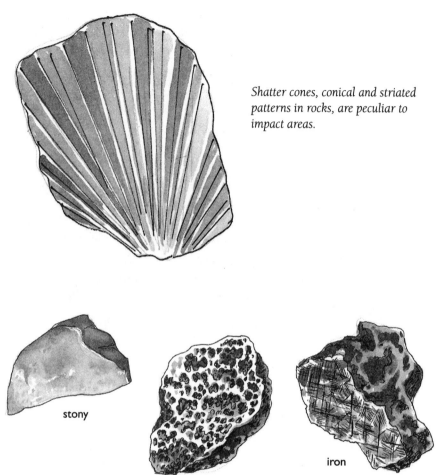

Shatter cones, conical and striated patterns in rocks, are peculiar to impact areas.

stony

stony iron

iron

Meteorites are classified into three groups. Most meteorites, perhaps 93 percent of those recovered, are stony meteorites, containing silica-rich minerals. Stony iron meteorites, the rarest (2 percent), contain both silica-rich minerals and nickel-iron alloys. Iron meteorites, constituting the final 5 percent of recovered meteorites, are composed of nickel and iron.

Tektites are the glassy remnants of molten material created by meteoritic impact and thrown into the air. Tektites are sometimes found scattered around impact craters.

surrounding rock has been melted by the high temperatures brought on by the meteoritic collisions. The melted materials contain abundant iridium from the meteorites, as well as layers of tiny round grains called spherules associated with recrystallization of minerals due to heat.

IMPACT STRUCTURES

Meteorite craters are not always easy to detect. Sometimes they are so large that their concentric structures are discovered only from satellite images. The world's largest known impact crater, centered on the city of Prague in the western Czech Republic, is at least 100 million years old and 200 miles (320 kilometers) in diameter. Its immense structure was detected from a weather satellite photograph. The presence of another significant impact structure, the Sudbury igneous complex in Ontario, Canada, was confirmed because of geological evidence: the presence of shatter cones, which are rocks fractured in conical and striated patterns, peculiar to impact areas. Also significant at Sudbury is the richness of nickel ore in the area. The area's igneous rocks were melted on impact by the meteorite, which may have been composed of a nickel-iron alloy. Upon impact, metals separated out of the melted igneous rocks, consolidating into ore bodies in the area of the crater.

Generally, earth's known impact craters range in size from a few feet to many miles in diameter. Shatter cones and shocked quartz may be found in

impact crater

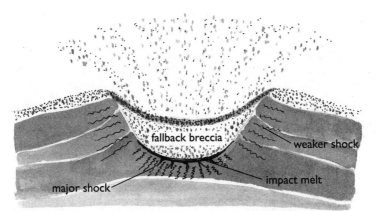

Impact craters have their own peculiar geologic structures, shown here in cross section. Existing layers of rock are disturbed by shock waves and impact melting. Material is ejected from the crater, including earthly rock and fragments of the meteorite that settle around the rim. Broken rock that falls back into the crater is called fallback breccia.

the rocks forming the crater. Coarse debris thrown up by the impact settles around the perimeter of the steeply banked rims, and surrounding sediments may be fused by heat into glassy spherules.

It is interesting to note that colliding extraterrestrial rocks were responsible for the formation of all the planets, including earth, making our life here possible. But rocks from space could end life on earth, too, as they have caused mass extinctions in the past. Astronomers differ in their opinions about how much danger asteroids pose to earth, and some maintain a constant asteroid watch. In their watch for near-earth asteroids, astronomers are attempting to detect when a large object is heading our way. If a major asteroid were bound for earth, they say, and we had five to ten years' lead time, we would probably have no choice but to prepare for the impact. But if we had fifty to one hundred years' notice, chances are we could design a rocket and well-placed chemical explosions that could divert the path of the earthbound object. Given the usual precision of the world's government space programs, such a diversion is entirely within our capabilities. The *Pioneer* spacecraft deployed to Saturn arrived only twenty seconds late after six years of travel. Astronomers believe that given proper lead time, we could probably hit a major asteroid and knock it off course. For now, however, we can only watch the skies. If necessary, we can prepare to shape geologic history by avoiding another catastrophic meteoritic event when the time comes.

TO DO

MAPPING SHOOTING STARS

What you will need

watch

flashlight

warm clothes

chair

photocopy of a star chart

notebook

You can conduct your own observation of near-earth meteoroids by mapping meteors, also known as shooting stars.

Pick a night that will have a meteor shower (a concentration of thirty or more meteors per hour). Such showers are most likely to occur around August

11 and December 13. You can check the sky watch portion of your local newspaper for information about meteor showers. Dress warmly and sit facing the direction the shower should come from (this information is also available through sky watch reports). Check the time you begin your observations. Whenever you see a meteor, make a mark in your notebook. At the end of an hour, count the marks. Did you see thirty or more meteors?

You can map the meteors on your photocopied star chart. Note where each meteor falls with respect to surrounding constellations, and draw a line from the point where it was first visible to the point where it burned out. Mark the leading edge of the line (the direction the meteor was traveling) with an arrowhead. After an hour, check your meteor arrows to see the general direction of travel.

Explanation: Most meteors are comet debris, pebble-sized pieces of rock that were once mixed with the ice of comets. These pieces were trapped in the comets when the solar system formed billions of years ago and subsequently were released. Some of these pieces become trapped in cometlike orbits and can remain so for centuries. For several nights each year, the earth encounters these streams of particles that have not yet dispersed at times that have remained constant over the years. We intercept each other when our orbits cross.

Meteor showers are named for the constellations from which they seem to be streaming, as indicated by the lines and arrowheads drawn on your star chart. The point at which all your meteor trails seem to begin is called the radiant, and it should indicate a constellation for which to name your shower.

MAKING CRATERS

What you will need

flour

large baking pan

powdered paint

marble, rubber ball, golf ball

tongs

ruler

string

scale

notebook

Create your own impact craters in a baking pan filled with flour.

In your notebook, write out a table like the one below.

Meteorite (Ball)	Ball Mass	Ball Diameter	Depth of Crater	Diameter of Crater	Notes
Golf ball					
Rubber ball					
Marble					

Cover the bottom of the pan with the flour, at least .5 inch (1.25 centimeters) deep. Sprinkle the surface of the flour with colored paint. Measure and weigh each ball, then drop each by turns into the flour from a chosen height. You may want to use the string to help you measure the dropping distance above the flour. Using tongs, remove the balls from their craters. Note the physical features of each crater and record all data in your chart. Repeat as often as you wish, preparing new flour beds when necessary. How does the size of the ball affect the size of the crater?

Explanation: Larger meteorites create larger impacts and larger craters.

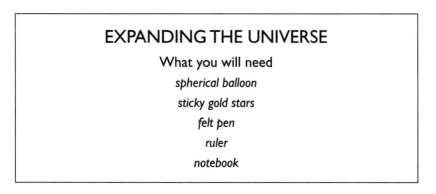

EXPANDING THE UNIVERSE
What you will need
spherical balloon
sticky gold stars
felt pen
ruler
notebook

You can use a balloon to illustrate how the universe has been expanding since the big bang.

Stick the gold stars to the balloon. Imagine that the stars are really galaxies—some close together, some widely separated. Cluster the galaxies in places and separate them in others. Measure the distances between some of the galaxies. Mark the distances in your notebook and, using the felt pen, mark each galaxy with a corresponding number on the balloon. Blow up the balloon but don't tie it off, as you may want to repeat the experiment. What happens to the galaxies when the balloon increases in size? Measure the distances between marked galaxies while the balloon is inflated. Note that the galaxies themselves do not expand and that no new ones are created.

Explanation: It may seem to us on earth that we are at the center of the universe. In truth, however, the universe has no center and no edges. All galaxies are simultaneously moving away from each other, as the expanding balloon illustrates. Galaxies across the balloon are moving not only away from each other but also from their closest neighbors. The farther apart two galaxies are, the faster they retreat from each other.

Expansion of the universe began with the big bang billions of years ago. The continued expansion we see today, the moving apart of galaxies, is a relic of that initial propulsion.

TO THINK ABOUT

Strings of Pearls. Comets as well as asteroids can collide with the earth and other planets, but comets are distinctive. Dubbed "dirty snowballs" by astronomer Fred Whipple in 1950, comets are mixtures of ice and dust. When forced out of their distant comet cloud from beyond our solar system by the gravity of stars, comets assume new, slow orbits around the sun. Then people all over the world take note of these remarkable visitors from out in space. Their sometimes spectacular appearance derives from the melting of their outer material, which grows into a huge cloud of dust and gas as its nears the sun.

Comets are named for whoever first spots them and reports them to official astronomical organizations. Comet Hyakutake, which attracted the world's attention in early 1996, was named for amateur astronomer Yuji Hyakutake, who discovered it with binoculars as he sat among mountains he had been climbing.

When comets collide with planets, they can create impact craters of their own. When a comet named Shoemaker-Levy 9 (the ninth comet named for astronomers Shoemaker and Levy) smashed into Jupiter's gaseous atmosphere in July 1994, it was called a string of pearls comet, broken into fragments before its collision. On earth, one confirmed chain of impact craters stretches like a similar string of pearls from southern Illinois, through central Missouri, into Kansas. The eight impact craters forming the chain may have been made by pieces of a shattered comet.

Recently scientists may have found another string of pearls, in Chad in central Africa. The presence of impact craters in Chad was first indicated in photographic images taken by the space shuttle *Endeavour* in April 1994. In April 1996, new spaceborne imaging radar detected signs of two additional craters near a known impact site in northern Chad. Scientists need to check the ground for evidence to confirm that the impressions are truly impact craters, but the initial findings are important: If confirmed, the string of pearls in Chad would be the first impact craters detected by a space-based radar system, deployed jointly by the United States, Germany, and Italy.

Radioactivity. Blasts from past meteoritic impacts are often compared to nuclear explosions in terms of their intensity. Scientists say that some impact blasts were probably comparable to the effects of millions of atomic warheads like those exploded over Hiroshima and Nagasaki at the end of World War II. The 1908 explosion over Siberia has been compared to the impact of eight hundred Hiroshima-type bombs; the force of the Cretaceous-Tertiary explosion of 65 million years ago was probably more than 10 million times greater than eight hundred Hiroshimas. We use the nuclear explosions in Japan as measures of comparison because they are the largest explosions we have yet seen. If past meteoritic blasts were indeed so much larger than the nuclear explosions of our experience, their effects are beyond comprehension.

One important difference between meteoritic blasts and nuclear explosions, however, is that the latter are accompanied by radioactivity. Meteoritic explosions are not caused by superpowerful reactions within the nuclei of atoms that in splitting release radiation. Many of the horrors inflicted on people in Hiroshima and Nagasaki were caused strictly by radiation. The meteoritic impacts of millions of years ago are not believed to have caused radiation sickness in the species of long ago, but simply to have caused explosions too immense to survive.

TO READ

Beiser, Arthur, and the editors of Time-Life Books. *The Earth.* New York: Time-Life Books, 1970. Another in the Time-Life series on natural phenomena, with excellent photographs and text.

Dickinson, Terence. *From the Big Bang to Planet X: The 50 Most-Asked Questions about the Universe . . . and Their Answers.* Camden East, Ontario: Camden House, 1993. Clear, fun-to-read explanations about the earth's place in space.

Moeschl, Richard. *Exploring the Sky: Projects for Beginning Astronomers.* Chicago:

Chicago Review Press, 1992. Fun activities help the reader understand everything from deep within the earth to out past the stars.

Popular Science Monthly editorial staff. *Everybody's Guide to Astronomy.* New York: Popular Science, 1934. Includes projects and experiments related to the planets.

Steel, Duncan. *Rogue Asteroids and Doomsday Comets.* New York: John Wiley & Sons, 1995. Tells of asteroids and comets gone astray from their celestial orbits.

TO WATCH

Life on Mars: The Water Connection. United States Geological Survey Open File Report 90-93B. United States Geological Survey, 1990. Film of a lecture and slide presentation about the Martian atmosphere.

Solar System Roulette: Consequences of Large Impact Events for Life on Earth. United States Geological Survey, 1988. Describes the chances of a large meteorite or comet hitting the earth.

GLOSSARY

aeolian. Wind deposited.

aquifer. Water-bearing underground layer of rock, sand, or gravel.

asteroid. One of many small celestial bodies in orbit around the sun, especially between the orbits of Mars and Jupiter.

batholith. Huge mass (more than 40 square miles or 100 square kilometers) of plutonic rock.

bedrock. Solid rock beneath loose overlying material such as soil.

biota. Animal and plant life of an area.

braided stream. A stream with an interlacing network of channels.

calcite. Most common mineral form of the compound calcium carbonate, found in limestone, chalk, and marble. Also a common rock cement.

caldera. Large, basin-shaped depression formed at the site of major volcanism. May contain several volcanic vents.

cast. Material filling a hole left by a fossil that has dissolved.

catastrophism. Notion that all the earth's features are formed by gigantic and sudden upheavals.

cement. Chemically precipitated, finely crystalline material that fills the spaces among the clasts of a sedimentary rock, binding them together.

clast. Grain or fragment of sediment.

cleavage. Splitting or preference to split along planes determined by a mineral's structure.

climatology. Study of the characteristic weather of a region.

conchoidal. Curved fracture occurring in substances that have no cleavage.

core. Central part of the earth, probably consisting of iron-nickel alloy.

crater. Basin-shaped structure on a volcanic cone; rimmed structure formed by the impact of a meteorite.

craton. Stable crust that forms the nucleus of a continental plate.

cross-bedding. Layers of sediment deposited at an angle to a horizontal bedding plane.

crust. Outermost layer of the earth, divided into continental and oceanic plates.

crystal. Solid formed by regularly repeating arrangement of atoms of a chemical element or compound. May have distinctive planar faces.

crystal form. Geometric shape of a crystal.

crystallize. Process by which elements are arranged in regularly repeating patterns in a crystal.

delta. Wedge-shaped accumulation of sediments at the mouth of a river.

dense. Characterized by compactness or close packing together of elements.

density. Mass of a substance per unit of volume.

deposition. Laying down of any rock-forming material primarily by wind or water.

diagenesis. Process of making rock from sediment through the action of compaction, cementation, and chemical changes.

dinosaur. Extinct subclass of land-dwelling reptiles.

elastic rebound. Theoretical process by which rocks abruptly release energy built by increasing strain between crustal blocks along a fault. Through rebound, the rocks are restored to a condition of little or no strain.

element. Substance that cannot be broken down into other substances.

epicenter. Point on the surface of the earth directly above the focus of an earthquake.

erosion. Wearing away of rock by the action of water, wind, and ice.

evolution. Theoretical process by which species change in form and function in response to changing environments.

extinction. Disappearance of a species so that it no longer exists anywhere.

extrusion. Process by which magma arrives at the earth's surface, usually through volcanic action.

facies, sedimentary. Distinct part of a rock or group of rocks that differs from the whole sedimentary formation by virtue of composition, age, or fossil assemblage.

fault. Break within the crust along which the crustal blocks on either side slide past each other.

focus. True center of an earthquake, at which seismic energy is first released.

fossil. Piece, impression, or trace of an organism of past geologic ages that has been preserved in rock.

gem. Precious (of great value) or semiprecious mineral. Often cut and polished.

geochronology. Study of time with respect to the history of the earth.

glacier. Mass of snow compacted into a body of ice that radiates out from its center or moves down a valley or slope.

gradient. Slope, particularly of a stream or ground surface.

groundwater. Underground water that supplies springs and wells.

hydrologic cycle. Cycle of change through which water passes, from vapor in the atmosphere to water through precipitation and ultimately back to vapor through evaporation and transpiration.

hydrothermal. Of or relating to hot water, its action, or minerals deposited from it.

igneous. Solidified from magma.

impact crater. See crater.

inclination. Angle of difference from horizontal or vertical.

inorganic. Not a living organism or derived from one; has no carbon in its internal structure.

intensity. Measure of the effects of an earthquake's shaking on people, their buildings and structures, and the earth's surface.

intrusion. Process by which magma pushes upward through the crust to solidify beneath the earth's surface. Also referred to as plutonism.

lahar. Landslide or mudflow of volcanic debris.

lava. Molten rock that issues from a volcano or crack in the earth.

law of original horizontality. Concept that sediments are deposited in horizontal layers, or beds, parallel or nearly parallel to ground surface.

law of superposition. Basic principle that within any given sequence of undisturbed sedimentary and volcanic rock layers, younger beds overlie older beds.

liquefaction. Process of making or becoming liquid or behaving like a liquid.

magma. Molten rock material generated within the earth.

magnetic poles. Points on the earth's surface with which magnetic forces are aligned. Not necessarily coincident with geographic north.

magnitude. Measure of the total energy released by an earthquake.

mantle. Semimolten interior of the earth between the core and crust.

matrix. Fine-grained material filling the spaces among larger clasts in a sedimentary rock.

meander. Sinuous curve of a stream.

metamorphic. Has undergone change in composition or texture effected primarily by pressure and heat.

mineral. Naturally occurring inorganic element or compound (neither animal nor plant) having an orderly internal structure and characteristic chemical composition, crystal form, and physical properties.

mold. Impression left in surrounding rock by a dissolved or removed fossil or fragment.

molten. Melted; liquefied by heat.

moraine. Accumulation of rock debris deposited by the direct action of glacier ice.

offset. Displacement of previously aligned features.

organic. Has carbon in its internal structure. Is either a living organism or derived from one.

paleoclimatology. Study of past weather patterns.

paleomagnetism. Faint orientation of magnetic particles within rocks polarized with respect to the earth's magnetic field at the time and place of rock formation.

paleontology. Study of ancient life.

permeability. Capacity of a rock or sediment layer to transmit liquids, depending on the size and shape of pores and their interconnections.

petrified wood. Wood that has been turned to stone by replacement of the original structure with silica.

planetesimals. Small celestial bodies in our early solar system, believed to have coalesced into the planets.

porosity. Percentage of a rock that consists of pores, or open space.

pyroclastic. Of or regarding material blasted from a vent by explosive volcanic activity.

recrystallization. Growth of new mineral grains in a rock while in the solid state.

rift zone. Spreading center from which continental or oceanic plates separate. Accompanied by extensive volcanism and formation of new crust.

rock. Mass composed of one or more minerals.

saturation. Degree to which the pores within a rock or sediments contain oil, gas, or water.

sediment. Solid material that has been transported and deposited by wind, water, or ice.

sedimentary. Formed by the settling or deposition of sediment.

seismic. Of or pertaining to earthquakes or earth vibrations, even if artificially induced.

seismograph. Instrument used to record earth vibrations.

silica. Chemical compound, silicon dioxide, that occurs in several forms, including quartz (crystals), opal (gel), and silica cement (submicroscopic crystals), and is a building block of many other minerals.

slope. Inclined part of any earth surface.

soil. Earth material that is so modified by erosion and weathering that it can support plant life.

Steno's laws. See law of original horizontality and law of superposition.

striation. One of multiple parallel grooves or lines formed either on a mineral surface through crystallization or on a rock surface through scratching or impact.

stromatolites. Fossil mounds of layered blue-green algae.

subduction. Process by which one crustal plate is pushed beneath another.

superheat. To heat above the vapor point without converting into vapor.

taphonomy. Study of the processes (decay, transport, and burial) affecting plant and animal remains between death and fossilization.

tectonic. Of or regarding the major structural or deformational geologic features and their origins, relations, and histories.

terrestrial. Earthlike. Terrestrial planets are like the earth, in terms of qualities like density and silica composition.

till. Nonsorted, nonstratified rock material deposited by a glacier.

tsunami. Great sea wave produced by seismic energy of an earthquake or volcanic eruption.

uniformitarianism. Principle that the present is the key to the past; thus past geologic activities can be explained on the basis of current geologic processes.

vapor. Substance in its gaseous, rather than solid or liquid, state.

vent. Opening at the earth's surface through which lava is extruded.

ventifact. Stone that has been changed or shaped by wind action.

RESOURCES

You can call or write the national organizations listed below to learn more about specific geologic resources in your area or about geology in general. Because researchers from all over the world contribute their expertise to these organizations, they have information on the most recent findings from expeditions in earth sciences. Most publish regular journals or magazines on the latest breakthroughs and interpretations by geologic researchers.

American Association for the Advancement of Science (AAAS)
1333 H Street, NW
Washington, DC 20005
(202) 326-6600

United States Geological Survey (USGS)
Geologic Inquiries Group
907 National Center
Reston, VA 22092

American Association of Petroleum Geologists (AAPG)
P.O. Box 979
Tulsa, OK 74101
(918) 584-2555

American Geological Institute
4220 King Street
Alexandria, VA 22302-1507
(800) 336-4764
(703) 379-2480

American Geophysical Union (AGU)
2000 Florida Avenue, NW
Washington, DC 20009
(800) 424-2488

The following national, state, and local organizations may have offices in your area. Look in your telephone book or check your local library for addresses and phone numbers. All are potential sources of information about earth sciences. Other local resources you might call or visit for information include the library, college and university geology departments, natural history museums, and rock and lapidary shops.

Association for Women Geoscientists

United States Geological Survey

United States Bureau of Land Management

United States Forest Service

State Bureau or Department of Mining and Geology

State Department of Water Resources

State Department of Forestry

You can find answers to specific geologic questions through on-line computer access to publications, databases at university departments, research laboratories, and government institutions. Check your on-line service's directory of searchable publications as well as its guide to the Internet. Most services post indexes to magazines you can browse using key words for your search. On the Internet, try using general search words such as geology, geography, fossils, astronomy, earth science, and planetary geology to find sites that contain documents, images, and files of interest to earth scientists. Then narrow your search according to your area of interest and see where it leads you. Although the telephone and your public library can still be the quickest and least expensive means to finding information, exploring on-line databases and publications also may be helpful.

SUPPLIES

The study of the earth requires your curiosity and powers of observation more than anything else, but you may want to buy tools and other books for your geologic activities and outdoor explorations. Call bookstores in your area and commercial businesses such as rock shops, sporting goods stores, hobby shops, and gift shops at nature centers. Or write the following organizations for catalogs (most places will send them free of charge and postage paid). Maps are available from most organizations listed here and are reasonably priced.

American Association for the Advancement of Science Books
Department 89A
P.O. Box 753
Waldorf, MD 20604

National Geographic Society
Educational Services Catalog
1145 17 St. NW
Washington, DC 20036
(800) 368-2728
(301) 921-1330

The Nature Company
P.O. Box 2310
Berkeley, CA 94702

Science Kit and Boreal Laboratories
777 East Park Drive
Tonawanda, NY 14150-6782 (*East Coast*)
or
P.O. Box 2726
Santa Fe Springs, CA 90670-4490 (*West Coast*)

The Smithsonian Institution
Department 0006
Washington, DC 20073-0006

United States Geological Survey
Map Distribution Center
1200 South Eads Street
Arlington, VA 22202
> *(for geologic and topographic maps of the United States east of the Mississippi River)*

United States Geological Survey
Map Distribution Center
Federal Center, Building 41
Denver, CO 80225
> *(for geologic and topographic maps of the United States west of the Mississippi River)*

Ward's Natural Science Establishment, Inc.
5100 West Henrietta Road
P.O. Box 92912
Rochester, NY 14692-9012 *(East Coast)*
or
11850 East Florence Avenue
Santa Fe Springs, CA 90670-4490 *(West Coast)*

World of Science
Merrell Scientific Division
1665 Buffalo Road
Rochester, NY 14624